D0909725

ESSENTIALS OF *Old English*

ESSENTIALS OF *Old English*

READINGS WITH KEYED GRAMMAR AND VOCABULARY

Constance B. Hieatt
ST. JOHN'S UNIVERSITY

THOMAS Y. CROWELL COMPANY
NEW YORK
Established 1834

Library of Congress Catalog Card Number: 68-13382

DESIGNED BY MARGARET F. PLYMPTON

MANUFACTURED IN THE UNITED STATES OF AMERICA

Preface

This book is an elementary descriptive grammar of Old English, based on reading exercises from Old English literature and taking into account word-frequency in Old English poetry. It is an introductory text, intended to provide students with a grasp of the grammatical structure and vocabulary of Old English sufficient for reading purposes in a minimum period of time. It does not attempt to cover the finer philological points: advanced students (and those whose primary interest is in Germanic philology) should continue their study using a comprehensive, or reference, grammar (see Suggestions for Further Study).

Students of any language are likely to prefer a direct approach through reading literature to an undiluted preliminary dose of declensions and conjugations, but they cannot construe unfamiliar sentence structures correctly until they have digested the basic grammatical signals. For this reason unfamiliar words, forms, and constructions are glossed in each selection, a standard English translation appearing directly above the Old English and, where it seems helpful, a more literal gloss above that. In the discussions that follow, various grammatical points illustrated in the reading are explained. Simpler grammatical topics are discussed in the first few chapters, with more complex matters reserved for a later stage. However, those who wish to unravel mysteries not yet explained may check in the Index to find where a particular point is discussed. Words listed in a Review Vocabulary at the end of a chapter are not glossed when they recur in a subsequent reading, but they are all included in the Complete Review Vocabulary, as are any recurring in a reading in a form which looks sufficiently different from their first occurrence to puzzle a beginner.

Reading selections have been chosen with several objects in view: ease and relative familiarity were primary considerations for the first few readings, while literary and historical interest took precedence for the later chapters. Since it seems clear that I am far from being alone in wishing my students to proceed to the poetry as soon as possible, the last selection includes Cædmon's Hymn. A brief note on the meter and rhythm of the poem (and Old English versification) is appended.

Another necessary consideration guiding the choice of readings was the grammatical features to be illustrated. For example, since the personal pronouns are so frequent as to be of first importance, it seemed advisable to use passages that would illustrate as many as possible in the first two selections. Vocabulary was another major factor. Here my prime objective was to provide the beginner with a useful basic vocabulary for reading poetry. For this reason, the words listed in the Review Vocabularies are all among those listed in the first fifteen pages of the Madden-Magoun *Grouped Frequency Word-List*: that is to say, these words, or their immediate relatives, all occur at least one hundred times in the corpus of Old English poetry. Almost all of the word groups listed among the first hundred in frequency are represented by at least one word in the Complete Review Vocabulary.

This principle of vocabulary selection has inevitably led to the omission from the Complete Review Vocabulary of a great number of common words (such as ***dohtor*** 'daughter') that happen not to occur one hundred or more times in the poetry. Many of these words (as is the case with ***dohtor***) have come down to Modern English in more or less unchanged form, and should be easily recognized; a number of them are listed in the Supplementary Vocabulary. Perhaps this section will be of help to those who are primarily interested in the history of the language; however, it is some way from being a comprehensive list, since it includes only words which have actually occurred in the reading selections.

Orthography presented some of the hardest decisions. In the

Old English field there is still no firm consensus on the subject of normalization, and even among those who agree that normalization is desirable—or indeed necessary—in elementary texts, there is disagreement about which stage of the language should be represented. The same disharmony prevails in the use of the alphabet. While few editors today cling completely to scribal practice ("wen," for example, is rarely found in modern texts), and most at least use some indication of vowel length, any group of texts selected at random is likely to show two or three different ways of writing the same word.

My own course in both matters is not that of any one previous editor, and perhaps for that reason will run the risk of striking everyone as unsatisfactory for different reasons. In general my spelling is close to that of John C. Pope in *Seven Old English Poems* (see Suggestions for Further Study), although in many ways it conforms to that used by J. F. Magoun and F. P. Madden and by J. B. Bessinger. The spelling is, then, Early West Saxon in many respects—notably the retention of ***ie***—but I have used ***e*** rather than ***œ*** for the i-mutation of ***o,*** and have preferred the later spelling of ***eo*** to Early West Saxon ***io.*** Since in some other respects I have preferred textual forms rather than theoretical restorations (for example, ***mé*** and ***þé*** have not been normalized to ***meċ*** and ***þeċ*** in the accusative), the forms in this text coincide in many respects with the Late West Saxon forms found in Quirk and Wrenn's *An Old English Grammar.*

The acute accent instead of the macron is used for vowel length; ***ȝ*** is used rather than ***ġ*** (or *g*) for the palatal *g*; ***þ*** is reserved for the voiceless initial and final consonant, and ***ð*** for the voiced sound. However, in the case of palatal *c,* I have preferred the appearance of the dotted ***c*** (***ċ***), which may help forestall possible confusion arising from the use of the acute accent to mean two quite different things.

Possibly the eclectic nature of this system of orthography may be in itself an advantage to the student, since the text thus has some features in common with almost any of the texts which are likely to be used for further work. For example, a student who goes on to use the Madden-Magoun *Grouped Frequency*

Word-List for vocabulary building while starting to read Pope's edition of some of the poems should have little difficulty in simultaneously adjusting to the two somewhat different systems—even if he is also using a reference grammar with still another variation. (Incidentally, it is with such situations in mind that I have grouped ***æ*** after ***a*** and ***þ*** after ***t*** in the alphabetized vocabulary listing; many more texts use some such system than list them separately at the end of the alphabet.) Of course, an instructor may wish his class to turn directly to unnormalized texts; in any case, the student should find enough that is familiar to orient himself quickly.

I am grateful to Professors Jess B. Bessinger and Robert P. Creed for helpful suggestions and criticisms given at various stages of the preparation of this book.

C.B.H.

Suggestions for Further Study

This bibliography is intended primarily for the student who is working on his own; no attempt has been made to be exhaustive, but, rather, to list a few selected works in each category.

Grammars

Brunner, Karl, *Altenglische Grammatik, nach der angel-sächsischen Grammatik von Eduard Sievers,* 3rd ed. Tübingen: Max Niemeyer, 1965. Referred to as "Sievers-Brunner."

Campbell, A., *Old English Grammar.* Oxford: Clarendon Press, 1959.

Quirk, Randolph, and C. L. Wrenn. *An Old English Grammar,* rev. ed. New York: Holt, Rinehart, and Winston, 1957. A convenient, concise volume, not an exhaustive treatment.

Readers containing reference grammars

Anderson, Marjorie, and Blanche Colton Williams, *Old English Handbook.* Boston: Houghton-Mifflin, 1935.

Bright's Anglo-Saxon Reader, rev. James R. Hulbert. New York: Henry Holt, 1935.

Moore, Samuel, and Thomas A. Knott, *The Elements of Old English,* rev. James R. Hulbert. Ann Arbor: George Wahr, 1955. Primarily a grammar.

Anthologies

Bolton, W. F., *An Old English Anthology.* Evanston: Northwestern University Press, 1966.

Fowler, Roger, *Old English Prose and Verse.* London: Routledge and Kegan Paul, 1966.

Magoun, F. P., Jr., *The Anglo-Saxon Poems in Bright's Anglo-Saxon Reader,* rev. ed. Cambridge, Mass.: Harvard University, Department of English, 1960. A normalized text; paperback.

Pope, John C., *Seven Old English Poems*. Indianapolis: Bobbs-Merrill, 1966. A normalized text, with a section on Old English versification; paperback.

Dictionaries, etc.

Bessinger, J. B., *A Short Dictionary of Anglo-Saxon Poetry*. Toronto: University Press, 1960.

Clark Hall, J. R., *A Concise Anglo-Saxon Dictionary*, 4th ed. with Supplement by Herbert D. Meritt. Cambridge: University Press, 1960.

Madden, John F., and F. P. Magoun, Jr., *A Grouped Frequency Word-List of Anglo-Saxon Poetry*. Cambridge, Mass.: Harvard University, Department of English, 1960. Paperback.

Contents

ESSENTIALS OF
Old English

CHAPTER 1

The Lord's Prayer

Fæder úre, þú þe eart on heofonum, síe þín nama ʒehálgod; tó-becume þín ríċe; ʒeweorðe þín willa on eorðan swá swá on heofonum; úrne ʒedæʒhwǽmlíċe hláf selle ús tó-dǽʒ; and forʒief ús úre gyltas, swá swá wé forʒiefaþ úrum gyltendum; and ne ʒelǽd þú ús on costnunge, ac álíes ús of yfele. Sóþlíċe.

1.1 This passage uses four letters not in the Modern English alphabet:

(a) the vowel *æ* (and its corresponding long sound, *ǽ*), called "ash";

(b) two consonants which represent the sounds spelled *th* in Modern English: ***þ***, "thorn" and ***ð***, "eth";

(c) ***ʒ***, "yogh"—the Old English *g* (for its use in this text, see section **1.6**).

1.2 Some letters of the Old English alphabet stand for more than one sound, notably ***c***, ***g*** (or ***ʒ***), and all the vowels and diphthongs. For this reason, many texts use a superscribed dot (***ċ, ġ***), acute accent (***ć, á, é***), or macron (***ā, ē***) to distinguish the sounds so marked from others (***c, g, a, e,*** etc.). See section **1.6** for a résumé of the sounds of Old English (hereafter abbreviated O.E.) and the spellings used in this book.

1.3 Most of the words above are still found in later English: ***Fæder*** 'Father'; ***úre*** 'our'; ***þú*** 'thou'; ***eart*** 'art' ('are,' 2nd person sing.); ***on*** 'on,' 'in'; ***heofon*** 'heaven'; ***þín*** 'thy' (cf. 'thine'); ***nama*** 'name'; ***ʒehalgod*** 'hallowed'; ***tó-becume*** 'come' (i.e., roughly, 'come to us'); ***willa*** 'will'; ***eorðe*** 'earth'; ***swá*** 'so,' 'as'; ***ʒedæʒhwǽmlíċe*** 'daily' (***dæʒ*** 'day' plus ***-líċe*** '-ly,' [***ʒe-***]***hwá*** meaning 'each'); ***hláf*** 'loaf' (bread); ***selle*** 'sell' (give); ***ús*** 'us'; ***tó-dæʒ*** 'today'; ***and*** 'and'; ***forʒief*** 'forgive'; ***gyltas*** 'guilts' (sins, trespasses); ***wé*** 'we'; ***ne*** 'not,' 'nor'; ***ʒelǽd*** 'lead'; ***álíes*** 'loose' (free, deliver); ***of*** 'of' (from); ***yfele*** 'evil'; ***sóþlíċe*** 'soothly' (in sooth, truly, amen).

1.4 Almost all of the words in this passage which have no obvious modern English derivatives do have modern German cognates: ***síe*** = *sei* 'be'; the prefix ***ʒe-*** = *ge-*; ***ríċe*** = *Reich* 'kingdom'; ***ʒeweorðe*** = *werde* 'become,' 'be done'; ***costnunge*** 'temptations,' from O.E. verb ***costian*** = *kosten* 'taste,' 'try,' 'make trial of.'

1.5 English shares with other Germanic languages a tendency to lose inflectional endings; thus O.E. had many inflections which have disappeared from Modern English (hereafter abbreviated Mod.E.). Examples may be seen above: ***úre,*** nominative case, but ***úrne,*** accusative, and ***úrum,*** dative; ***forʒief,*** imperative singular, but ***forʒiefaþ,*** 1st person indicative plural. The sooner the beginner can recognize these inflections, the less difficulty he will have with O.E. vocabulary.

1.6 Guide to O.E. pronunciation

I. Vowels

	O.E.	Phonetic (IPA)	Like	In	In O.E.	Mod.E. trans.
A. *Back, or guttural*						
1. low	***a***	ɑ	o	mop	***mann***	man
	á	ɑ:	a	mar	***mán***	crime
2. mid	***o***	ɔ	o	more	***scop***	minstrel
	ó	o:	o	mote	***scóp***	created
3. high	***u***	u	oo	moor	***full***	full
	ú	u:	oo	moot	***fúl***	foul
B. *Front, or palatal*						
1. low	***æ***	æ	a	mat	***mæʒ***	may (verb)
	ǽ	æ:	a	math	***mǽʒ***	kinsman
2. mid	***e***	ɛ	e	met	***westan***	from the west
	é	e:	a	mate	***wéstan***	lay waste
3. high	***i***	ɪ	i	mitt	***lim***	limb
	í	i:	ee	meet	***lím***	lime
C. *Mixed, high*						
	y	y	ü (Ger.)	Mütter	***ryne***	running
	ý	y:	ü (Ger.)	Mühler	***rýne***	secret
D. *Diphthongs*[1]						
	ea	æə or ɛə			***ʒeare***	readily
	éa	æ:ə or ɛ:ə			***ʒéar***	year
	ie	ɪə			***hierde***	guardian
	íe	i:ə			***híerde***	heard
	eo	eo			***seonu***	sinew
	éo	e:o			***séon***	see
	io[2]	ɪo			***ʒioguþ***	youth
	ío[2]	i:o			***ʒío***	formerly

[1] In diphthongs, both vowel sounds are heard, but pronounced as a single glide. (No Mod.E. equivalents can be given—there are none.)

[2] Early West Saxon; later ***eo, éo***. The ***eo, éo*** spellings are more usual in O.E. literary texts, for which reason they are the preferred spellings in this book.

II. Consonants: most as in Mod.E.; e.g., ***b, d, l, m, n, p, t.***

BUT

A. There are no silent letters; e.g.:

1. double consonants are both pronounced (***bb*** in ***habban*** 'have' is like *bb* in *grab-bag*, not as in *grabbing*).
2. ***ng,*** as in ***singan*** 'sing,' is pronounced as in *finger*, not as in *singer*.
3. ***cniht*** 'youth' has four consonant sounds, not two as in Mod.E. *knight*.

B. The spirants ***f, s, þ,*** and ***ð*** are:

1. voiceless (*f* as in *fat*, *s* as in *soon*, *th* as in *thin*)
   (a) initially and finally, as in ***sóna*** 'soon,' ***fæder*** 'father,' ***þanc*** 'thought,' ***áþ*** 'oath,' ***stæf*** 'staff.'
   (b) when doubled or before voiceless consonants, as in ***siþþan*** 'since,' ***fæst*** 'firm.'
2. voiced (*v* as in *over*, *z* as in *prize*, *th* as in *then*) medially (except as in 1b above, or at the beginning or end of elements of compounds), as in ***ofer*** 'over,' ***rísan*** 'rise,' ***eorðe*** 'earth.' [3]

C. O.E. ***g*** (***ʒ***) and ***c*** represent several sounds:

1. palatal (*y* as in *yield*, *ch* as in *church*), usually before or after front vowels, as in ***ʒeaf*** 'gave,' ***dæʒ*** 'day,' ***ċild*** 'child,' ***iċ*** 'I.'
2. gutteral (*g* as in *good*, *k* as in *keep*), usually before or after back vowels, as in ***gód*** 'good,' ***dagas*** 'days,' ***cyning*** 'king,' ***ac*** 'but.' [4]
3. ***cg*** is the palatal sound spelled *dg* in Mod.E., as in ***brycg*** *bridge*, ***secgan*** 'say.'
4. ***sc*** is almost always the sound spelled *sh* in Mod.E., as in ***scip*** *ship*, ***fisc*** 'fish.'

[3] Note that in this text, ***þ*** is used for the voiceless sound and ***ð*** for the voiced sound, although O.E. scribes did not consistently differentiate these letters.

[4] In this text, *ʒ* represents the palatal *g* and ***g*** the guttural; palatal *c* is indicated by a dot (*ċ*).

D. O.E. ***h*** has two sounds:

1. *h* as in *hand* before vowels: ***hand*** 'hand,' ***hús*** 'house.'
2. *ch* as in German *ich* and *ach* before consonants and after vowels: ***dohtor*** 'daughter,' ***néah*** 'near,' ***hwæl*** 'whale.'

III. Accentuation: the first syllable is stressed, unless it is an unemphatic prefix (like ***ȝe-***, ***be-***, ***á-***): ***dohtor, inweardlíċe, déaþstede;*** but ***wiþstandan, árisan, bebod.***

EXERCISES

A. Locate further examples of inflected endings in the Lord's Prayer (aside from those cited in section **1.5**).

B. Practice reading the Lord's Prayer aloud after studying the guide to pronunciation. For further practice in the pronunciation of Old English, listen to a record made by an expert and repeat the words in the indicated pronunciation. Among the records which can be recommended are *Beowulf, Caedmon's Hymn and Other Old English Poems,* read by J. B. Bessinger, Jr. (Caedmon Records, TC 1161); *Lyrics from the Old English,* read by Burton Raffel and Robert P. Creed (Folkways Records, FL 9858); and *Selections from Beowulf,* read by John C. Pope (Lexington, LE 5505).

CHAPTER 2

From *The Ten Commandments*

Deuteronomy 5:6–15

TRANSLATED BY ÆLFRIC

I am (the) Lord your God
Iċ eom Dryhten éower God. . . .

Nor name ye
Do not take (the) Lord's name in
Ne nemne ʒé Dryhtnes naman on

for that *nor is he*
vain because he is not guiltless
ídel, for-þon þe ne biþ hé unscyldiʒ,

his name calls
who for (a) vain purpose takes his name
sé þe for ídelum þinge his naman nemþ.

Hold *rest-day*
Keep the sabbath-day
Heald þone reste-dæʒ,

you *it* *hallow*
(so) that you hallow it as (the) Lord
þæt þú hine halgiʒe swá Dryhten

he *and thus said*
commanded saying Work
hé bebéad, and þús cwæþ: "Wyrċ

six days and rest (on) the
siex dagas and freolsa þone

seventh Remember that you (your)selves
seofoðan." Ʒemunaþ þæt ʒé selfe

were in bondage in the land of Egypt and
wǽron þéowe on Egypta lande and

you released
I delivered you
iċ éow álíesde.

Honor your father and your
Árweorða þínne fæder and þíne

mother (so) that you (may) be long-lived
módor, þæt þú síe lang-lífe,

and (so) that you (may) be prosperous in the
and þæt þú síe weliʒ on þǽm

you to give wishes
land that God wishes to give you
lande þe God þé sellan wile.

Not be you *man-slayer*
Do not be a murderer
Ne béo þú mann-slaga.

Do not commit adultery
Ne unriht-hǽme þú.

Do not steal
Ne stel þú.

say
Do not bear false witness
Ne sæȝe þú léase ȝewitnessa.

Do not covet your neighbor's wife
Ne ȝiern þú þínes néahstan wífes,

none
nor his land nor any (of) the things
né his landes, né nán þára þinga

his *be*
that are his
þe his béoþ.

2.1 In the reading selections of the first two chapters occur various forms of five personal pronouns: ***iċ*** 'I' (1st per. sing.); ***þú*** 'thou' (2nd per. sing.); ***hé*** 'he' (3rd per. sing.); ***wé*** 'we' (1st per. pl.); and ***ȝe*** 'you,' 'ye' (2nd per. pl.). *Paradigm*[1] of the 1st and 2nd person forms, singular and plural, (bracketed forms have not yet occurred in readings):

[1] In a *paradigm* (i.e., a sample of the pattern of forms) of a noun, pronoun, or adjective, each position in the column (up and down) indicates the set of relationships we call *case*, the form used for a particular grammatical function.

	Singular		Plural	
Nom.[2]	***iċ***	***þú***	***wé***	***ʒé***
Gen.	[***mín***]	***þín***	***úre***	***éower***
Dat./acc.	[***mé***]	***þé***	***ús***	***éow***

[2] The following abbreviations are used in paradigms throughout: nom.—nominative (subject form); gen.—genitive (possessive); dat.—dative (indirect object and various relationships expressed by prepositional constructions in Mod.E.); acc.—accusative (direct object).

2.2 It will be noted that in Selection 2 ***hine,*** acc. of ***hé,*** is translated 'it' rather than 'him,' since its antecedent is the noun *day*. In O.E. ***dæʒ*** is masculine, not neuter. The genders of O.E. nouns are not dependent on sex: ***hús*** 'house' is neuter, but ***hám*** 'home' is masculine; ***wiht*** 'creature,' 'being' is feminine, but ***wíf*** 'woman,' 'wife' is neuter; ***wæl*** 'slaughter' is neuter, but ***déaþ*** 'death' is masculine.

2.3 Two masculine nouns in the selection appear in two forms: ***dryhten*** (nom. sing.), ***dryhtnes*** (gen. sing.), and ***dæʒ*** (acc. sing.), ***dagas*** (acc. pl.). These nouns belong to a set of forms that, in O.E., can be organized in a pattern similar to that of the personal pronoun, above. This pattern is called a paradigm of a declension.[3]

Dryhten and ***dæʒ*** belong to the strong masculine declension. Almost identical with it is the strong neuter declension, to which two of the nouns in this passage belong: ***þing*** 'thing,' 'business,' and ***land*** 'land,' both here in the dative singular (***þinge, lande***).

2.4 Paradigms of the strong masculine and neuter declension of nouns: ***hám*** 'home,' ***dæʒ*** 'day,' ***dryhten*** 'lord' (m.); ***land*** 'land,' ***ríċe*** 'kingdom,' ***wæl*** 'slaughter' (n.):

[3] We "decline" a noun by stating the case forms necessary to indicate grammatical functions. Thus, a noun *declension* is a group of nouns which use the same case forms. Forms showing cases other than the nominative are referred to as *inflected*.

	Masculine			Neuter			Endings
			Singular				
Nom./acc.	***hám***	***dæʒ***	***dryhten***	***land***	***ríċe***	***wæl***	-
Gen.	***hámes***	***dæʒes***	***dryhtnes***[5]	***landes***	***ríċes***	***wæles***	***-es***
Dat.	***háme***	***dæʒe***	***dryhtne***	***lande***	***ríċe***[7]	***wæle***	***-e***
			Plural				
Nom./acc.	***hámas***	***dagas***[4]	***dryhtnas***	***land***[6]	***ríċu***	***walu***[4]	***-as; -, -u***
Gen.	***háma***	***daga***	***dryhtna***	***landa***	***ríċa***	***wala***	***-a***
Dat.	***hámum***	***dagum***	***dryhtnum***	***landum***	***ríċum***	***walum***	***-um***

[4] ***a*** becomes ***æ*** (palatalizing a following ***g***) except when ***a, o,*** or ***u*** follows in the next syllable.

[5] Disyllabic nouns ending in a consonant usually drop the vowel of the second syllable in inflected forms.

[6] Neuter strong noun forms differ from the masculine only in nominative/accusative plural: ***-u*** in many words; long-stemmed monosyllables are uninflected in nominative/accusative plural. N.B.: a syllable is long when its vowel or diphthong is long or when it is ended by a long (spelled doubled) consonant or a consonant cluster.

[7] Strong nouns regularly have ***-e*** in dative singular; but nouns ending in ***-e*** do not add another.

2.5 Note that adjectives are also declined; e.g., in this passage: ***on <u>ídel</u>*** (acc. sing.); ***for <u>ídelum</u> þinge*** (dat. sing.); cf. also ***þone <u>seofoðan</u>*** [*dæʒ*] (acc. sing.). (The declension of adjectives is somewhat different from that of nouns, and will be taken up in a later chapter.)

2.6 Among the verbs which have occurred in Chapters 1 and 2 are several forms of the verb ***béon*** (past: ***wesan***) 'to be,' which is, as in all other Indo-European languages, common, important, and irregular. So far, the following forms have occurred: ***þú eart*** 'thou art,' ***þú síe*** 'thou (may) be'; ***iċ eom*** 'I am,' ***hé biþ*** 'he is,' ***ʒé wǽron*** 'you were,' ***beoþ*** 'are,' ***síe*** and ***beo*** 'be' (imperative). Paradigm[8] of the present indicative forms:

[8] We "conjugate" a verb by stating the endings, or inflections, necessary to differentiate between persons, tenses, etc. Thus, the pattern of forms of a group of verbs which use the same inflections is called a paradigm of a *conjugation*.

(*iċ*) ***béo, eom*** (*þú*) ***bist, eart*** (*hé*) ***biþ, is***
(*ȝé*) ***béoþ, sint, sindon, earon***

Note that there are at least two forms for every person.

REVIEW OF BASIC VOCABULARY FROM CHAPTERS 1 AND 2[9]

NOUNS

Masculine	Feminine	Neuter
dæȝ day	***eorðe*** earth	***hús*** house
déaþ death	***wiht*** creature, being	***land*** land
dryhten lord		***þing*** business, thing
fæder father		***wæl*** slaughter, corpse
hám home		***wíf*** woman, wife
heofon (also ***heofone*** [f.]) heaven		***yfel*** evil
nama name		
willa will, wish		

PRONOUNS

ic, þú, etc.: cf. section **2.1**

ADJECTIVES

ídel vain, worthless, empty ***lang*** long ***sóþ*** true
weliȝ prosperous

ADVERBS

sóþlíċe truly[10] ***swá*** so, as

[9] All words in Review Vocabularies should be learned: they will not be glossed again. To find explanations of forms which have not yet been discussed, check in the Index.

[10] Note that adverbs frequently consist of an adjective plus the ending ***-líċe*** '-ly.' Similarly (as in Mod.E.) a noun plus ***-líc*** becomes an adjective. In subsequent vocabularies, only the base form (i.e., noun or adjective) will be listed in such cases.

PREPOSITIONS

for for, on account of ***on*** in, on ***of*** from, of

CONJUNCTIONS

ac but ***and*** and ***for-þon*** because (also adv.) ***þæt*** that, so that (sometimes appears as ***þætte***)

VERBS

béon be (cf. section **2.6**) ***cwæþ*** (he) said

EXERCISES

A. Decline ***dǽl*** 'part' and ***engel*** 'angel' (m.) and ***þing*** (n.).

B. Can you identify by its form a masculine noun in Chapter 2 which does *not* belong to the strong declension?

CHAPTER 3

Creation

Genesis 1:1–5

TRANSLATED BY ÆLFRIC

created God
(the) beginning God created
On anᵹinne ᵹescóp God heofonan

The was
and eorðan. Séo eorðe sóþlíċe wæs ídel

darknesses were
empty darkness was over the
and ǽmtiᵹ, and þíestra wǽron ofer þǽre

abyss's broadness
surface of the abyss spirit
niwelnesse brádnesse, and Godes gást

carried (the) waters then
wæs ᵹeferod ofer wæteru. God cwæþ þá:

become *became*
Let there be light was
''Ʒeweorðe léoht.'' And léoht wearþ

made saw it was good
ʒeworht. God ʒeseah þá þæt hit gód wæs;

divided the from the
and hé ʒedǽlde þæt léoht fram þǽm

called the
þíestrum, and hét þæt léoht dǽʒ and

became
the night Then made
þá þíestra niht. Þá wæs ʒeworden

one day
(the) evening morning (of the) first day
ǽfen and morgen án dæʒ.

then again Let there be now
God cwæþ þá eft: ''Ʒeweorðe nú

(a) firmament in the midst (of) the waters
fæstness tó-middes þǽm wæterum, and

separate the
tótwǽme þá wæteru fram þǽm wæterum.''

made
And God ʒeworhte þá fæstnesse, and

were under
tótwǽmde þá wæteru þe wǽron under

the those which
þǽre fæstnesse fram þǽm þe wǽron

above then
bufan þǽre fæstnesse. Hit wæs þá

called
swá ʒedón. And God hét þá fæstnesse

made evening
heofonan. And wæs þá ʒeworden æfen

morning (of the) second day
and morgen óðer dæʒ.

3.1 The words ***séo, þǽre, þæt*** in ***þǽt léoht, þǽm,*** and ***þá*** in ***þá þíestra*** have all been glossed as 'the' (in one case, 'those'). These are some of the forms of the definite article, or demonstrative pronoun, which must agree in gender, number, and case with the noun it modifies. In the masculine and neuter singular, it also has an additional case form not given for nouns: instrumental. Instrumental forms of nouns are identical with the dative, and for that reason are not listed separately. (The instrumental case is used to denote agency, means, or instrument.)

3.2 Paradigms of the definite article:

	Singular			
	Masculine	Feminine	Neuter	Endings
Nom.	***sé***	***séo***	***þæt***	***-, -, -t***
Gen.	***þæs***	***þǽre***	***þæs***	***-s, -re, -s***
Dat.	***þǽm***	***þǽre***	***þǽm***	***-m, -re, -m***
Acc.	***þone***	***þá***	***þæt***	***-ne, -, -t***
Ins.	***þý/þon***	***þǽre***	***þý/þon***	***-[n], -re, -[n]***

Plural, all genders

Nom./acc.	***þá***	**-**
Gen.	***þára***	***-ra***
Dat./ins.	***þǽm***	***-m***

3.3 Note that the genitive and dative singular forms of the masculine and neuter articles are identical (in the same way, as already indicated, genitive and dative singular endings of masculine and neuter strong nouns are identical). But the feminine article differs from the masculine and neuter articles in these cases. In the same way, the genitive and dative singular endings of feminine strong nouns differ from the equivalent masculine and neuter strong noun endings. Also, like the genitive and dative singular forms of the feminine article, the genitive and dative singular endings of feminine strong nouns are identical. Feminine strong nouns in Selection 3 include ***brádness*** 'broadness,' 'surface.'

3.4 Most of the O.E. nouns which do not belong to the strong declensions are called "weak nouns" and have a declension of their own. This includes all masculine nouns with nominative singular ending in ***-a;*** all feminine nouns with nominative singular in ***-e;*** and a very few neuters with nominative/accusative singular ending in ***-e.*** Among the weak nouns in the reading selections so far are ***nama*** and ***willa*** (m.) and ***eorðe*** (f.).

3.5 Paradigms of the strong feminine declension and the weak declension of nouns: ***lár*** 'learning,' ***sáwol*** 'soul' (f. strong); ***nama*** (m.), ***éage*** 'eye' (n.), and ***eorðe*** (f.) weak:

	Strong feminine		Endings	Weak			Endings
			Singular				
Nom.	***lár***[1]	***sáwol***	***-, -u***	***nama***	***éage***	***eorðe***	***-a, -e***
Acc.	***láre***[2]	***sáwle***[4]	***-e, -***	***naman***	***éage***[5]	***eorðan***	***-an, -e, -an***
Gen./dat.	***láre***	***sáwle***	***-e***	***naman***	***éagan***	***eorðan***	***-an***
			Plural				
Nom./acc.	***lára***[3]	***sáwla***	***-a, -e***	***naman***	***éagan***	***eorðan***	***-an***
Gen.	***lára***	***sáwla***	***-a, -ena***	***namena***	***éagena***	***eorðena***[6]	***-ena***
Dat.	***lárum***	***sáwlum***	***-um***	***namum***	***éagum***	***eorðum***[7]	***-um***

[1] Some short-stemmed monosyllables add ***-u*** as nominative singular feminine ending; cf. nominative plural of strong neuter nouns.

[2] Some long-stemmed feminine monosyllables lack ***-e*** in accusative singular.

[3] ***-a*** and ***-e*** are alternative nominative/accusative plural endings for feminine strong nouns, but ***-a*** is most frequent except for some long-stemmed monosyllables.

[4] ***a*** becomes ***æ*** except when ***a, o,*** or ***u*** follow in the next syllable (cf. p. 10, footnote 4).

[5] Neuter forms are always the same in nominative/accusative.

[6] All nouns end in ***-a*** in genitive plural; for weak nouns and as an alternative form for strong feminine nouns, the ***-a*** is preceded by ***-en: -ena.***

[7] The dative plural of all nouns, regardless of declension, is ***-um.***

3.6 Two more forms of the verb ***béon/wesan*** occur in this passage: ***wæs*** 'was' (3rd per. sing., past); and ***wǽron*** 'were' (3rd per. pl., past). Note that in the past the 3rd person plural is the same as the 2nd person plural (cf. section **2.6**). This is because the past indicative plural ending is the same for all persons in all verbs: it is always ***-on.*** Paradigm of the past indicative forms of ***béon/wesan:***

(***iċ***) ***wæs*** (***þú***) ***wǽre*** (***hé***) ***wæs***
(***wé, ʒé***) ***wǽron***

REVIEW VOCABULARY

NOUNS

Masculine	Feminine	Neuter
gást spirit, soul, ghost	***lár*** learning	***anʒinn*** beginning
	niht night	***éage*** eye
God God	***sáwol*** soul	***wæter*** water

PRONOUNS

hit it ***þe*** who, which, what ***sé, séo, þæt*** (definite article): cf. section **3.2**

ADJECTIVES

án one ***gód*** good ***midd*** middle; cf. ***tó-middes*** ***oðer*** second, other

ADVERBS

eft again, after, back ***nú*** now ***þá*** then

PREPOSITIONS

fram from, by ***ofer*** over ***under*** under

EXERCISES

A. Decline ***heofone, niht,*** and ***willa.***

B. Identify the number and case of the following words in the contexts specified in Selection 3: ***Godes; dæʒ*** in ***hét þæt léoht dæʒ; dæʒ*** in ***án dæʒ; anʒinne; wæteru.***

CHAPTER 4

From King Alfred's Preface to the *Cura Pastoralis*

bids to be greeted
Alfred (the) king greets Warferth
Ælfréd cyning háteþ grétan Wærferþ,

(in) words lovingly and friendly
his bishop (in) loving and friendly terms
biscop his, wordum luflíċe and fréondlíċe,

thee to know bids
bids you know (to) me (has) come very often
and þé cýðan háte þæt mé cóm swíðe oft

mind what wise men formerly were
on ʒemynd hwelċe witan ʒéo wǽron

English race
throughout England
ʒeond Angel-cynn . . . .

this all remembered
Then when I remembered all this
Þá iċ þá þis eall ʒemunde, þá

wondered I very greatly
I was very much astonished at good
wundrode iċ swíðe swíðe þára gódena

wise men who
witena þe ʒéo wǽron ʒeond Angel-cynn,

by full learned had
all the books had fully learned
and þá béċ ealla be fullan ʒeleornod hæfdon,

of them not any part did not wish
they did not wish to turn any part of them into their
þæt híe hira þá nǽnne dǽl noldon on hira

to turn
own language at once
ágen ʒeþéode wendan. Ac iċ þá sóna eft

me myself answered
answered myself They
mé selfum andwyrde and cwæþ: ''Híe

ever men should
did not think men would ever
ne wéndon þætte ǽfre menn scolden

so reckless become
become so reckless learning
swá reċċeléase weorðan, and séo lár

because of their will
decline intentionally
swá oþfeallan; for þǽre wilnunga

they left it undone wished here
híe hit forléton, and woldon þæt hér

were *in that we*
more wisdom (the) would be the
þý mára wísdóm on lande wǽre þý wé

more we knew
má ʒeþéode cúðon.''

4.1 The pronoun or adjective '*this*' is about as common in O.E. as in Mod.E.: e.g., above in the phrase ***iċ þis ʒemunde.*** It is declined in some respects like ***sé*** and in some like a strong noun:

	Singular		
	Masculine	Feminine	Neuter
Nom.	***þés***	***þéos***	***þis***
Gen.	***þisses***	***þisse***	***þisses***
Dat.	***þissum***	***þisse***	***þissum***
Acc.	***þisne***	***þás***	***þis***
Ins.	***þýs***	***þisse***	***þýs***

Plural, all genders	
Nom./acc.	***þás***
Gen.	***þissa***
Dat./ins.	***þissum***

4.2 In the passage above the nouns ***béċ*** (f.) and ***menn*** (m.) are obviously plural, but lack the usual plural endings, weak or strong. They belong to a small group of common nouns which have a change of vowel owing to mutation in the stem of the dative singular and nominative/accusative plural, rather than endings for these cases. This declension includes ***burg*** 'city' (f.). Paradigms of ***mann*** and ***burg:***

	Singular		Plural	
Nom./acc.	***mann***	***burg***	***menn***	***byriȝ***
Gen.	***mannes***	***byriȝ***	***manna***	***burga***
Dat.	***menn***	***byriȝ***	***mannum***	***burgum***

4.3 The verb ***noldon*** 'they did not wish' is the negative form of ***woldon,*** which appears later in the same passage. Many O.E. words have such negative forms beginning with ***n-*** (i.e., a contraction with ***ne***): ***nǽnne*** < ***nán*** = ***ne án;*** there are many others, such as ***nǽfre*** = ***ne ǽfre.*** N.B.: double negatives are frequent in O.E.: 'they didn't want to translate none of them.'

4.4 There are a number of verbs in the past tense in this passage, most of which end in ***-d*** plus personal endings such as ***-e*** or ***-on.*** A suffix of ***-d, -t, -ed,*** or ***-od*** in the past tense is characteristic of the verbs classified as *weak,* of a small group of important irregular verbs classified as *preterite* (i.e., past)-*present* (PP), and of most of the even smaller (and even more important) group of irregular verbs classified as *anomalous* (A). ***Woldon*** (past ind. pl. of ***willan***) is an anomalous verb; the others are ***dón*** 'do' (the past participle, ***ȝedón,*** appeared in Chapter 3); ***gán*** 'go,' and ***béon.*** Preterite-present verbs in the passage above are ***ȝemunde*** (past ind. 3rd per. sing. of [***ȝe-***]***munan***)[1]; ***cúðon*** (past ind. pl. of ***cunnan***); and ***scolden*** (past subjunctive pl. of ***sculan***). Forms of preterite-present and anomalous verbs will be discussed in later chapters.

4.5 Weak verbs are classified in three groups. Those of class I form the past tense and past participle by adding ***-ed, -d,*** or ***-t*** to the stem of the infinitive. The infinitive itself

[1] Many verbs have prefixes which have little or no effect on meaning and do not regularly appear; ***ȝe-*** is the most frequent.

usually ends in ***-an*** (in a few cases ***-ian***). Class II verbs have ***-ian*** in the infinitive and ***-od*** in the past indicative and past participle. Class III verbs are somewhat irregular in appearance. Among the weak verbs in the passage above are ***wénan*** (I) 'expect,' 'think'; (***ʒe-***)***leornian*** (II) 'learn'; and ***habban*** (III) 'have.' Other very common weak verbs include ***séċan*** (I) 'seek'; ***þenċan*** (I) 'think'; ***lufian*** (II) 'love'; and ***libban*** (III) 'live.' The principal parts of representative verbs are:

	Infinitive	Past ind. 1st per. sing.	Past part.
I	***séċan***	***sóhte***	***sóht***
II	***lufian***	***lufode***	***lufod***
III	***habban***	***hæfde***	***hæfd***

4.6 The past indicative endings for weak verbs are ***-e*** in the 1st and 3rd persons singular, ***-est*** in the 2nd person singular, and (like all other verbs—cf. section **3.6**) ***-on*** in the plural, all persons. Thus the complete paradigm of ***séċan*** in the past indicative is:

(***iċ***) ***sóhte*** (***þú***) ***sóhtest*** (***hé***) ***sóhte***
(***wé, ʒé, híe***) ***sóhton***

REVIEW VOCABULARY

NOUNS

Masculine	Feminine	Neuter
cyning king	***burg*** city	***cynn*** race, kin
dæl part	***lufu*** love	***word*** word
fréond friend		
mann man		
wísdóm wisdom		
wita wise man, counselor		

PRONOUNS

híe they ***þés, þéos, þis:*** cf. section **4.1**

ADJECTIVES

ágen own ***eall*** all (also pron.) ***hwelċ*** which, what (also pron.) ***full*** full (also adv.) ***má, mára*** more ***nán*** no (also pron.: none) ***self*** self, same ***wís*** wise

ADVERBS

ǽfre ever ***hér*** here ***nǽfre*** never ***oft*** often ***sóna*** at once, soon ***swíðe*** very, greatly

CONJUNCTIONS

þá . . . þá then . . . when

PREPOSITIONS

ȝeond throughout ***be*** by

VERBS

(Cf. sections **4.4–5;** included here are important weak verbs from Chapters 1–4)

I: ***cýðan*** make known, tell
(ȝe-)dǽlan divide, give out
(ȝe-)ferian carry, bring
(ȝe-)lǽdan lead
(á-)líesan free, loose, deliver
séċan (***sóhte, sóht***) seek
sellan (***sealde, seald***) give, sell
þenċan (***þóhte, þóht***) think
wénan expect, think
wendan turn, return, translate
wyrċan (***worhte, worht***) work, make

II: (*ʒe-*)***halgian*** hallow, make holy
lufian love
wundrian wonder

III: ***habban*** have
libban (***lifde, lifd***) live

PP: ***cunnan*** know
(*ʒe-*)***munan*** remember, consider
sculan shall, have to

A: ***dón*** do
gán go

EXERCISES

A. Conjugate the past tense indicative of ***sellan.***

B. Why is it "obvious" that ***béċ*** is plural in the context above?

CHAPTER 5

From *The Anglo-Saxon Chronicle* for the Year 1066

year when he was king,
On þissum ȝéare . . . þe hé cyning wæs,

fared *ship-army*
went out with (a) fleet against
he fór út mid scip-here tóȝéanes

William meanwhile came Earl Tosti
Willelme; and þá hwíle cóm Tostiȝ eorl

into (the) Humber
intó Humbran mid 60 scipum.

Earl Edwin force
Eadwine eorl cóm mid land-fierde and

boatmen
drove sailors
dráf hine út; and þá butse-carlas hine

forsook
forsócan, and hé fór tó Scotlande mid

small boats met
12 snaccum, and hine ȝemétte Harald sé

Norwegian
Norrena cyning mid 300 scipum, and Tostiȝ

one
submitted (to) they
him tóbéah. And man cýðde Harolde

how it was there done and come to pass
what had been done and had befallen there
cyning hú hit wæs þǽr ȝedón and ȝeworden,

(a) large army
and hé cóm mid miċlum here Engliscra

[Harald] at Stamford
manna and ȝemette hine æt Stængfordes

Bridge slew
brycge and hine ofslóg, and þone eorl

courageously
Tostiȝ, and eallne þone here éhtlíċe

overcame
ofercóm. And þá hwíle cóm Willelm

up
ashore Hastings
eorl upp æt Hestingan on Sancte

Michaelmas
Michæles mæsse-dæȝ; and Harold cóm

from the north fought against him before
norðan and him wið feaht ǽr-þon

fell
þe his here cóme eall; and þǽr hé féoll,

two brothers Gyrth
and his twéȝen ȝebróðra Gyrþ and

Leofwin conquered
Léofwine, and Willelm þis land ȝeéode,

and cóm tó Westminstre, and Ealdréd

archbishop consecrated
arcebiscop hine tó cyninge ȝehálgode,

paid gold hostages
and menn guldon him gold and gíslas

after(wards)
sealdon, and siþþan hira land

bought
redeemed
bohton . . . .

5.1 Another form of the personal pronoun occurs in this passage: ***him*** (dat. sing. [and pl.] 3rd per.). Paradigm of the 3rd person personal pronouns (including the feminine singular forms, which have not yet been illustrated in the readings):

	Singular			Plural
	Masculine	Feminine	Neuter	All genders
Nom.	***hé***	***héo***	***hit***	***híe***
Gen.	***his***	***hire***	***his***	***hira***
Dat.	***him***	***hire***	***him***	***him***
Acc.	***hine***	***híe***	***hit***	***híe***

Note the resemblance of the declension of the 3rd person personal pronoun to that of the definite article (demonstrative pronoun—cf. section **3.2**); e.g., in both cases the accusative singular feminine is identical with the nominative/accusative plural.

5.2 The noun ***ʒebróðra*** (m.) is clearly nominative plural, but does not have a regular masculine plural ending, strong or weak; ***bróðor*** belongs to another minor noun declension, which includes several nouns of relationship ending in ***-r,*** including ***fæder*** (m.) and ***sweostor*** 'sister' (f.). ***Fæder,*** the most common of these nouns, is declined like a masculine strong noun except that it has no ending for the nominative, accusative, or dative singular, and often also lacks an ending in the genitive singular and nominative/accusative plural.

5.3 Many verbs in the past tense in this passage are obviously not weak verbs since they do not have the weak past suffix. These are strong verbs, which form the past tense and past participle by a change in the vowel of the stem itself. This change is known as *ablaut;* there are seven ablaut series, and thus seven classes of strong verbs. Within each series, the original vowel changes were perfectly regular, but this is not always immediately apparent because of various sound changes (affecting some vowels in certain positions) before or during the O.E. period (cf. Chapter 10).

5.4 Six of the seven classes of strong verbs are represented in the passage above: (1) ***drífan*** 'drive'; (2) ***tóbúgan*** 'submit to,' from ***búgan*** 'bow'; (3) ***weorðan*** 'become' and ***ʒieldan*** 'pay'; (4) ***cuman*** 'come'; (6) ***faran*** 'go' and ***forsacan*** 'forsake,' from ***sacan*** 'fight'; (7) ***feallan*** 'fall,' 'die.' A common verb of class 5 is ***cweðan*** 'say,' which has occurred in Chapters 2, 3, and 4. (Note that infinitives regularly end in ***-an,*** like those of most weak verbs.) Among the strong verbs that have appeared in earlier chapters are: (5) ***forʒiefan*** 'forgive,' from ***ʒiefan*** 'give'; (7) ***hátan*** 'call,' 'name,' and ***healdan*** 'hold.' Other very common verbs include: (1) ***ʒewítan*** 'depart'; (3) ***beorgan*** 'conceal,' 'protect'; (5) ***sittan*** 'sit'; and (7) ***wealdan*** 'wield,' 'rule.'

5.5 Principal parts of representative verbs from this group are:

	Infinitive	Past ind. 1st per. sing.	Past ind. pl.	Past part.	Basic ablaut
1:	***ʒewítan***	***ʒewát***	***ʒewiton***	***ʒewiten***	***í, á, i, i***
2:	***búgan***	***béag***	***bugon***	***bogen***	***éo, éa, u, o***[1]
3:	***weorðan***	***wearð***	***wurdon***	***worden***	***e, a, u, u***[2]
4:	***cuman***	***cóm***	***cómon***	***cumen***	***e, æ, ǽ, o***[3]
5:	***cweðan***	***cwæþ***	***cwǽdon***	***cweden***	***e, æ, ǽ, e***
6:	***faran***	***fór***	***fóron***	***faren***	***a, ó, ó, a***
7:	***feallan***	***féoll***	***féollon***	***feallan***	"x, z, z, x"[4]

[1] A verb conforming exactly to the basic ablaut is ***béodan*** 'command.'

[2] Owing to sound changes (cf. Chapter 10), no verb conforms exactly to the basic class 3 ablaut. Close in different ways are ***bindan*** (***band, bunden, bunden***) 'bind,' and ***breʒdan*** (***bræʒd, brugdon, brogden***) 'brandish.'

[3] A verb conforming exactly to the basic ablaut is ***beran*** 'bear.'

[4] These verbs are called "reduplicating": they have various vowels in present and past participle, but all have either ***é*** or ***éo*** in the past tense forms; thus the pattern is always "x, z, z, x," with "x" being ***a, á, ǽ,*** etc., and "z" always either ***é*** or ***éo.***

5.6 The past indicative singular 1st and 3rd person forms are identical (as are those of weak verbs); the 2nd person singular adds the ending ***-e*** to the *plural* stem. Thus the past tense of ***beran*** (4) is:

(***iċ***) ***bær*** (***þú***) ***bǽre*** (***hé***) ***bær***
(***wé, ʒé, híe***) ***bǽron***

REVIEW VOCABULARY

(Includes strong verbs from Chapters 1–5;
cf. section **5.5** for forms where not given)

NOUNS

Masculine	Feminine	Neuter
eorl noble warrior, earl	***hwíl*** time, while (***þá hwíle*** meanwhile)	***gold*** gold

ADJECTIVES

miċel large, much ***twéʒen*** two

ADVERBS

ǽr before (also conj.) ***hú*** how ***þǽr*** there ***upp*** up, upwards ***út*** out

PREPOSITIONS

æt at ***intó*** into ***mid*** with ***tó*** to ***wiþ*** against

CONJUNCTIONS

ǽr-þon before ***siþþan*** after

VERBS

1: ***ʒewítan*** go, depart
2: (***be-***)***béodan*** command
búgan bow

3: ***beorgan*** (***bearg, burgon, borgen***) conceal, protect
ʒieldan (***ʒeald, guldon, golden***) pay
weorðan become, happen

4: ***beran*** bear
cuman come

5: ***cweðan*** say
ʒiefan (***ʒeaf, ʒéafon, ʒiefen***) give
(***ʒe-)séon*** (***seah, sáwon, sewen***) see
sittan (other forms regular) sit

6: ***faran*** go
forsacan forsake
sacan fight
(***ʒe-)scieppan*** (other forms regular) create, make

7: ***feallan*** fall
forlǽtan (***-lét***) forsake; ***lǽtan*** permit
hátan (***hét***) call, name
healdan (***héold***) hold
wealdan (***wéold***) wield, rule

EXERCISES

A. Conjugate the past indicative forms of ***faran***.

B. Did Harold kill Tosti, or vice versa? What grammatical signal makes this clear at once?

CHAPTER 6

From Ælfric's *Colloquium*

children ask O
PUPIL: ***Wé ċildru biddaþ þé, éala***

teacher teach to speak in
láréow, þæt þú tǽċe ús sprecan on

(the) Latin language correctly because
Léden ʒereorde rihte, for-þon

ignorant we are
we are ignorant
unʒelǽrede wé sindon, and

corruptly we speak
we speak corruptly
ʒewemmedlíċe wé sprecaþ.

what will you say
what do you want to say
MASTER: ***Hwæt wille ʒé sprecan?***

what do we care what we say

PUPIL: ***Hwæt réċe wé hwæt wé sprecan,***

correctly said be and properly

unless it is correctly and properly spoken

búton hit riht spréc síe and behéfe,

(is) not worthless or useless

næs ídel oþþe fracúþ?

Do you wish to be

MASTER: ***Wille ȝé béon***

in learning

beaten in order to learn

beswungen on leornunge?

we would rather

PUPIL: ***Léofre is ús béon beswungen***

know

for láre þænne hit ne cunnan; ac wé witon

merciful to be

to be merciful not to want to inflict

þé bilewitne wesan, and nellan onbelǽdan

whips (on) us unless are too compelled

swingla ús búton þú béo tó ȝeníedd

by

fram ús.

ask do you talk (about)

MASTER: ***Iċ áscie þé, hwæt spricst þú?***

have you of work
work do you have
Hwæt hæfst þú weorces?

(a) professed monk
PUPIL: ***Iċ eom ʒeanwyrde munuc,***

sing each seven times
and iċ singe ǽlċe dæʒ seofon tída mid

(the) brothers occupied reading
ʒebróðrum, and iċ eom bisʒod on rǽdinge

song nevertheless
and on sange; ac þéah hwæðere iċ

would between learn to speak
want to learn to speak
wolde betwénan leornian sprecan

in the Latin language between times
on Léden ʒereorde.

do these know
MASTER: ***Hwæt cunnon þás,***

your companions
þíne ʒeféran?

some are plowmen some
PUPIL: ***Sume sint ierþlingas, sume***

shepherds oxherds
scéap-hierdas, sume oxan-hierdas, sume

also likewise hunters fishermen
éac swelċe huntan, sume fisceras, sume

fowlers merchants
fugeleras, sume ċéap-menn, sume

shoemakers salters bakers
scó-wyrhtan, sealteras, bæceras.

say plowman
MASTER: ***Hwæt sæȝest þú, ierðling? Hú***

find
begǽst þú þín weorc?

dear lord hard
PLOWMAN: ***Éala, léof hláford, þearle iċ***

labor go at daybreak driving
deorfe; iċ gá út on dæȝ-rǽd, þýwende

oxen (the) field yoke (the) plow
oxan tó felda, and ȝeocie híe tó sýl.

It is not (ever) severe winter dare
Nis hit swá stearc winter þæt iċ durre

lie (hidden) fear
lútian æt hám, for eȝe mínes hláfordes;

(with) yoked oxen fastened
ac ȝeȝeocodan oxan and ȝefæstnodum

plowshare coulter plow each
sceare and cultre mid þǽre sýl, ǽlċe dæȝ

must plow (a) acre or
iċ sceal erian fulne æcer oþþe mára.

6.1 More present tense forms of ***béon, wesan*** appear in this passage, as well as the negatives ***næs*** and ***nis*** (***ne*** plus ***wæs*** and ***is***). Paradigm of ***béon, wesan:***

Indicative

		Present	Past
Sing.	(***iċ***)	***béo, eom***	***wæs***
	(***þú***)	***bist, eart***	***wǽre***
	(***hé***)	***biþ, is***	***wæs***
Pl.	(***wé, ʒé, híe***)	***béoþ, sint, sindon, earon***	***wǽron***

Subjunctive

	Present	Past
Sing., all pers.	***béo, síe, wese***	***wǽre***
Pl., all pers.	***béon, síen***	***wǽren***

6.2 This selection, since it is a conversation, has a great many verbs in the present tense. Among those in the present indicative are the 1st person singular of ***áscian*** (II)[1] and ***singan*** (3): ***iċ ascie, iċ singe;*** the 2nd person singular of ***sprecan*** (5) and ***habban*** (III): ***þú spricst, þú hæfst;*** and the 1st person plural of ***biddan*** (5) and ***sprecan*** (5): ***wé biddaþ, wé sprecaþ.*** Both 1st person singular forms end in ***-e;*** both 2nd person singular forms end in ***-st;*** the 1st person plural forms end in ***-aþ.*** These forms are almost universal for the present forms of all verbs, weak or strong (with the partial exception of ***béon,*** which conforms to few rules, and of some contract verbs—cf. section **8.4**). But there are some differences, nevertheless, between strong and weak verb endings in the present indicative.

[1] Pronounced *ask-*.

6.3 In general, to form the present indicative forms of verbs, drop the ending of the infinitive (***-an*** or ***-ian***) and add:

		Weak I & strong	Weak II	Weak III
Sing.	1st per.	***-e***	***-ie***	***-e***
	2nd per.	***-est***	***-ast***	***-ast***
	3rd per.	***-eþ***	***-aþ***	***-aþ***
Pl.	All pers.	***-aþ***	***-iaþ***	***-aþ***

6.4 Note the following facts about these forms: (a) The present indicative singular endings are ***-e, -st, -þ.*** (b) The plural (all persons) ends in ***-aþ,*** just as the past indicative plural always ends in ***-on.*** (c) *But* the situation is complicated by the fact that ***e*** appears before the ***-st*** and ***-þ*** of the singular endings in the case of strong and of weak I verbs, while ***a*** appears in this position for the others; also, the ***-e*** of the 1st person singular and the ***-aþ*** of the plural are preceded by ***i*** in weak II verbs only; the 3rd person singular of weak II and III verbs is identical with the plural forms of strong and weak I and III verbs.

6.5 Many forms are not quite as regular as might appear from **6.3.** For example, a great many strong verbs have "syncopated" present forms: thus we see, in the selection above, ***spricst*** instead of ***sprecest.*** Weak III verbs have their peculiarities: the 2nd person form of ***habban*** as given above is ***hæfst*** rather than ***habbast.*** As has already been noted (section **4.5**), ***gán*** is an anomalous verb. The 1st person present indicative, as illustrated above, is ***gá.***

6.6 Note that the infinitive is used much as it is in Mod.E.: ***tǽċe ús sprecan*** 'teach us to speak'; ***iċ wolde leornian sprecan*** 'I want to learn to speak.' Participles are also used in verb constructions in the same way as in Mod.E.: ***þú béo ʒeníedd*** 'you are compelled,' ***beón beswungen*** 'to be beaten,' ***iċ eom bisʒod*** 'I am occupied.'

REVIEW VOCABULARY

NOUNS

Masculine	Feminine	Neuter
eʒe fear	***tíd*** time, season	***weorc*** work
hláford lord		***winter*** winter (also pl.: years)
ʒeféra companion		
sang song		

PRONOUN

hwæt what

ADJECTIVES

éac also ***léof*** dear (***ús is léofre*** we would rather) ***súm*** some, (a) certain (also pron.) ***riht*** right, correct (also adverb: ***rihte***[2])

ADVERBS

swelċe likewise (also adj.: such, which) ***tó*** too

CONJUNCTIONS

búton unless, but ***hwæðer*** whether (also pron.: which) ***oþþe*** or ***þænne*** than ***þéah*** though; with ***hwæðere,*** nevertheless (also adv.)

VERBS

I: ***lǽran*** teach
secgan (***sæʒde***) say

[2] Like ***-líċe, -e*** is an ending often added to adjectives to make an adverbial form.

II: (***ʒe-)fæstnian*** fasten, secure
3: ***singan*** sing
5: ***biddan*** ask, pray
sprecan speak, say
7: ***rǽdan*** (***réd***) advise, read
PP: ***witan*** know

Note: From here on, principal parts of verbs will be noted only when they vary from the basic pattern for their group. Thus, past indicative of ***secgan*** is given, since it would be difficult to deduce it from the infinitive, but not of ***singan,*** since it shows the normal ablaut series for class 3 verbs: ***sang, sungon, sungen.***

EXERCISES

A. Conjugate the present and past indicative forms of ***lǽran*** and ***singan.***

B. Study the list of names of occupations (plowmen, shepherds, etc.) in the reading selection; deduce the declension of each of these nouns (and its nominative singular form). Some are compounds: can you find the separate words of which they are made? (What is the word for 'sheep,' for instance?)

CHAPTER 7

From *The Harrowing of Hell*

Gospel of Nicodemus

terribly
Hit wæs swíðe angríslíċe þá þá

Hell's lord
Satanas, þǽre Helle ealdor and þæs

commander
déaðes here-toga, cwæþ tó þǽre Helle,

prepare can Christ
"Ʒeʒearwa þé selfe þæt þú mæʒe Crist

receive glorified has
onfón, sé hine selfne ʒewuldrod hæfþ,

son
and is Godes sunu and éac mann, and éac

dreading
sé déaþ is hine ondrǽdende, and mín

sad (it) seems (to) me
sáwol is swá unrót þæt mé þynċþ þæt

live can
iċ álibban ne mæʒ. For-þon hé is miċel

antagonist against
wiðerwinna, and yfel wyrċende onʒeʒn

many
mé and éac onʒeʒn þé. And fela þe iċ

have controlled drawn
hæfde tó mé ʒewield and tó átogen—

blind lame crippled
blinde and healte, ʒebíeʒede and

leprous draws
hréoflan—ealle hé fram þé átíehþ.''

fiercely
Séo Hell þá swíðe grimme and swíðe

terribly answered
eʒeslíċe andswarode þá Satanase, þǽm

old devil
ealdan déofle, and cwæþ, ''Hwæt is sé þe

strong mighty if
is swá strang and swá mihtiʒ, ʒief hé

mann is, þæt hé ne síe þone déaþ

dreading we (two) long ago enclosed
ondrǽdende þe wit ʒefyrn beclýsed

have
hæfdon? For-þon ealle þá þe on eorðan

power might
anweald hæfdon, þú híe mid þínre mihte

draw firmly
tó mé ʒetuge, and iċ híe fæste ʒehéold.

And ʒief þú swá mihtiʒ eart swá þú ǽr

Savior
wǽre, hwæt is sé mann and sé Hǽlend þe

ne síe þone déaþ and þíne mihte

know if
ondrǽdende? Ac tó sóðum iċ wát ʒief hé

human nature
on menniscnesse swá mihtiʒ is þæt hé

neither us (two)
nǽðer né unc né þone déaþ ne ondrǽdeþ,

know
þæt iċ wát, þæt swá mihtiʒ hé is on

divine nature
godcundnesse þæt him ne mæʒ nán þing

withstand
wiþstandan. And iċ wát ʒief sé déaþ hine

then fights
ondrǽdeþ, þanne ʒeféohþ hé þé, and

eternal *world*
(to) you (shall) be woe eternity
þé biþ ǽfre wá tó éċere weorolde."

7.1 The pronouns ***wit*** and ***unc*** are dual forms—i.e., they are used instead of the plural ***wé*** and ***ús*** when only two people are referred to. Paradigms of the dual pronoun forms:

	Nom.	Gen.	Dat./acc.
1st per.	***wit***	***uncer***	***unc***
2nd per.	***ʒit***	***incer***	***inc***

7.2 The interrogative pronoun ***hwæt*** has a masculine form, ***hwá,*** which we might expect to find in the context above (***Hwæt is sé*** and ***hwæt is sé mann***); ***hwæt*** is the neuter form. There are no feminine or plural forms; the other (singular) forms are like those of ***sé, þæt***—i.e., ***hwæs*** (gen.), ***hwǽm*** (dat.), ***hwone*** (m. acc.), ***hwý, hwon*** (ins.). Another interrogative, ***hwelċ,*** is always declined as an adjective (cf. section **8.1–2**).

7.3 Some of the verbs in the passage above appear in subjunctive or imperative forms. These forms have already been noted in the case of ***béon*** (cf. sections **2.6** and **6.1**): note use of ***síe*** (pres. subj.) in the passage above. Another present subjunctive form is illustrated by ***mæʒe.*** The subjunctive endings, both present and past, are ***-e*** in the singular and ***-en*** in the plural for all verbs, with the usual exceptions in the case of ***béon*** and a few contract verbs which look much like it in the present subjunctive: e.g., ***séo, séon,*** from ***séon,*** 'see' (cf. ***béo, béon***).

7.4 The imperative, as illustrated above by ***ȝeȝearwa,*** ends in ***-a*** for weak verbs II and III. However, there is no ending for strong, anomalous, and long-stemmed weak I verbs: thus the imperative forms of ***beran*** (4), ***dón*** (A), and ***wendan*** (I) are ***ber, dó,*** and ***wend.*** Other weak I verbs have an imperative ending in ***-e,*** as do preterite-present verbs.[1]

7.5 The verb form ***wát,*** above, looks like the past indicative of a strong 1 verb, yet is glossed in the present 'know.' This is because ***witan*** is a preterite-present verb: the verbs of this group have present forms which were originally the past forms of strong verbs, and have weak past forms based on the present (originally past) stem. Principal parts of preterite-present verbs which have been listed in Review Vocabularies above (e.g., for Chapter 4), plus ***magan*** 'can,' 'may' (in the reading selection for this chapter) and ***ágan*** 'possess,' 'own,' are as follows:

Infinitive	Pres. ind. 1st per. sing.	Pres. ind. 2nd per. sing.	Past ind. 1st per. sing.
ágan	***áh***	***áhst***	***áhte***
cunnan	***cann***	***cannst***	***cúðe***
magan	***mæȝ***	***meaht/miht***	***meahte/mihte***
munan	***man***	***manst***	***munde***
sculan	***sceal***	***scealt***	***scolde***
witan	***wát***	***wást***	***wisse/wiste***

7.6 Paradigm of ***ágan:***

Pres. ind. (***iċ***) ***áh*** (***þú***) ***áhst*** (***hé***) ***áh***
(***wé, ȝé, híe***) ***ágon***

Pres. subj. sing. ***áge***

[1] There is also a plural imperative form, ending in ***-aþ*** (occasionally ***-an***) for almost all verbs.

Past ind. (*iċ*) ***áhte*** (*þú*) ***áhtest*** (*hé*) ***áhte***
(*wé, ʒé, híe*) ***áhton***

Past part. ***ágen***

Note: The present is like the past of strong verbs except for the 2nd person singular; the present plural and subjunctive and past participle use the same stem as the infinitive; the past indicative uses the regular weak endings; the past participle uses the strong ending ***-en.***

REVIEW VOCABULARY

NOUNS

Masculine	Feminine
ealdor lord	***hell*** hell
Hǽlend Savior	***miht*** might
sunu son	(***an-***)***weald*** power, control
	weorold world

PRONOUNS

hwá who (cf. section **7.2**) ***wit, ʒit*** we, you (two) (cf. section **7.1**)

ADJECTIVES

eald old ***eċe*** eternal ***grimm*** fierce, grim ***mennisc*** human ***mihtiʒ*** mighty ***strang*** strong

ADVERBS

fæste firmly ***þanne*** then (also conj.)

CONJUNCTION

ʒief if

VERBS

I: ***þynċan*** (***þúhte***) seem
(ʒe-)wieldan rule, control
II: ***ʒearwian*** make ready, prepare
(ʒe-)wuldrian glorify
3: ***winnan*** fight
6: ***standan*** (***stód***) stand
wiþstandan withstand
7: ***(on-)fón*** (***féng***) grasp, take
PP: ***ágan*** possess, own
magan can, be able to

EXERCISES

A. Conjugate ***cunnan*** in the present and past indicative.

B. To what other words in the passage above is the adjective ***mihtiʒ*** related? Can you draw any conclusions about word formation in O.E. from this group?

CHAPTER 8

St. Gregory and the Slave Boys

From Ælfric's *Homily on St. Gregory the Great*

perceived pope
þá underʒeat sé pápá, þe on þǽm

time apostolic seat possessed
tíman þæt apostolíċe setl ʒesæt, hú sé

blessed Gregory holy might(s)
éadiʒa Grégórius on hálgum mægnum

prospering
þéonde wæs, and hé þá hine of þǽre

monastic way of life took
munuclíċan drohtnunge ʒenam and him

as (a) helper placed deaconhood
tó ʒefylstan ʒesette, on díaconháde

ordained
ȝeendebyrdne.

happened occasion
þá ȝelamp hit æt sumum sǽle, swá

(it) still very often does English
swá ȝíet for oft déþ, þæt Englisce

merchants brought wares
ċeap-menn bróhton hira ware tó

Rome went along
Rómana-byriȝ, and Grégórius éode be

street
þǽre strǽt tó þám Engliscum mannum,

looking (at)
hira þing scéawiende. þá ȝeseah hé

among boys for sale placed
betwux þǽm warum ċiepe-cnihtas ȝesette

(of) white body fair
þá wǽron hwítes líċhaman and fæȝeres

appearance with splendid hair
andwlitan menn and æðellíċe ȝefeaxode.

beheld boys' beauty
Grégórius þá behéold þára cnapena wlite,

inquired nation brought
and befræȝn of hwelċre þéode híe ȝebróhte

someone
wǽron. Þá sǽȝde him man þæt híe of

England
Englalande wǽron and þæt þǽre þéode

people beautiful
mennisc swá wlitiȝ wǽre.

Eft þá Grégórius befræȝn hwæðer

people Christian heathen
þæs landes folc crísten wǽre oþþe hǽðen.

Him man sǽȝde þæt híe hǽðene wǽron.

(in his) inward heart
Grégórius þá of inweardre heortan

long-lasting sighs drew
langsume siċetunge téah, and cwæþ,

Alas color
"Wáláwá, þæt swá fæȝeres híewes menn

dark devil subject
sindon þǽm sweartan déofle underþéodde!"

asked what the name of the nation
Eft hé ascode hú þǽre þéode nama

was that they came of answered
wǽre þe híe of cómon. Him wæs ȝeandwyrd

Angles named
þæt híe Angle ȝenemnode wǽron. Þá

cwæþ hé, "Rihtlíċe híe sint Angle

angels' beauty
ȝehátene, for-þon þe híe engla wlite

befits
habbaþ, and swelċum ȝedafenaþ þæt híe

on heofonum engla ȝeféran béon."

8.1 Note that some of the adjectives in this selection have endings similar to those of strong nouns, while others have those of weak nouns; for example, ***sweartan,*** modifying ***þǽm deofle,*** is clearly a weak dative, while ***langsume*** bears the same strong dative ending as the noun it modifies. In the first case the article precedes the adjective, while in the other it does not. Generally, the weak declension of adjectives is used after any demonstrative or possessive pronoun and in direct address, while the strong declension is used (particularly in prose) in other circumstances.[1] Thus, for example, the dative plurals ***hálgum*** and ***Engliscum*** in this passage can be seen to be, respectively, strong and weak (which are in this case, of course, identical in form).

8.2 However, the endings of the strong declension of adjectives are not always identical with those of strong nouns, as may be observed from the forms above of ***Englisce*** (m. acc. pl.), ***hwelċre*** (f. sing. dat.), and ***sumum*** (m. sing. dat.). In such cases it can be seen that the strong declension of adjectives

[1] The ordinal numbers—e.g., ***forma*** 'first'—are declined as weak adjectives, while the first three cardinal numerals—***án, tweȝen,*** and ***þríe***—are declined as strong adjectives. Other cardinal numerals are not usually declined at all.

is more closely patterned on that of pronouns (cf. sections **3.2** and **5.1**), in that:

a. masculine dative singular ends in ***-um,*** not ***-e;***
b. masculine accusative singular ends in ***-ne;***
c. feminine genitive/dative singular end in ***-re,*** not ***-e;***
d. masculine nominative/accusative plural end in ***-e,*** not ***-as;***
e. genitive plural ends in ***-ra,*** not ***-a.***

Other points to be noted are that the feminine nominative singular and neuter nominative/accusative plural use the ending ***-u*** only on short stems, just as in the case of strong nouns, and that inflected forms of disyllabic adjectives ending in consonants, as in the case of nouns, often drop the vowel of the second syllable: e.g., ***hálgum*** (dat. pl. of ***háliȝ***).

8.3 Note that participles may be declined as adjectives (cf. above ***ȝeendebyrdne*** [m. acc. sing.]), but are often uninflected when used as predicate adjectives or appositives: e.g. above, ***þéonde,*** present participle of the contract verb ***þéon,*** and ***scéawiende,*** which has the usual present participle ending of ***-ende.*** (Cf. ***ondrǽdende*** and ***wyrċende*** in Chapter 7.)

8.4 *Contract verbs,* like ***þéon,*** have been mentioned before as exceptions to various rules (sections **6.2, 7.3, 8.3**). These irregularities were caused by the loss of an original ***-h*** from the stem of certain strong verbs, thus bringing the two vowels together to contract into one long vowel or diphthong: e.g., ***fóhan*** > ***fón; sehan*** > ***séon.*** The present tense, imperative, and present participle all show irregularities resulting from contraction. The present indicative 1st person singular of ***fón,*** for example, is ***fó.***

8.5 The noun ***Angle*** clearly does not belong to either of the main declensions: it represents another minor declension, which, however, is declined like the strong nouns except for the masculine nominative/accusative plural. Other important nouns belonging to this group include ***wine*** 'friend,' ***léod***

'people,' ***ielde*** 'men,' 'people,' and various names of peoples (e.g., ***Dene*** 'Danes').

8.6 This declension and those discussed earlier (sections **4.2, 5.2**) by no means complete the roster. Among the other minor declensions is that to which ***sunu*** and ***hand*** (f.) 'hand' belong. Its peculiarity is that masculine and feminine inflection is identical: ***-u*** in the nominative/accusative singular for all short-stemmed nouns; genitive/dative singular and nominative/accusative plural end in ***-a.*** Some other declensions differ from normal strong noun forms mainly in that there is usually no ending for the nominative/accusative plural; e.g., the declensions to which belong ***hæle*** or ***hæleþ*** (m.) 'hero,' 'man,' and ***féond*** (m.) 'enemy' (and ***fréond***), which has alternative nominative/accusative plural forms of ***fíend*** and ***féondas.***

REVIEW VOCABULARY

NOUNS

Masculine	Feminine	Neuter
andwlita face, appearance	***hand*** hand	***folc*** people, nation
engel angel	***heorte*** heart	***mægen*** might, power
féond enemy	***léod*** nation, people	***setl*** seat, residence
hæle/hæleþ man, hero	***þéod*** nation, people	
ielde men, people		
wine friend, benefactor, lord		

PRONOUN

man one, they (impersonal)

ADJECTIVES

ǽðele noble ***éadiʒ*** wealthy, blessed ***fǽʒer*** fair, beautiful

háliȝ holy ***inweard*** inward ***langsum*** long lasting ***wlitiȝ*** beautiful

ADVERB

for (usually an intensive prefix) very

VERBS

I: (***ȝe-***)***andwyrdan*** answer
(***ȝe-***)***bringan*** (***bróhte***) bring
(***ȝe-***)***nemnan*** name
(***ȝe-***)***settan*** set, place
3: (***be-***)***friȝnan*** (***fræȝn, frugnon, frugnen***) inquire
4: ***niman*** (***nam, námon, numen***) take
5: ***ȝesittan*** sit, possess, inhabit
underȝietan (***ea, éa, ie***) perceive, understand; more common form is ***onȝietan*** perceive.
7: ***behealdan*** (cf. ***healdan***) behold

EXERCISES

A. The Plowman in Chapter 6 says that he drives his oxen ***tó felda.*** What is the explanation of the form of ***felda?***

B. Give the gender, number, and case of the following adjectives as they appear in the selection above: ***éadiȝa, Englisce, munuclíċan, inweardre, hǽðen.***

CHAPTER 9

From Wulfstan's *Sermo Lupi ad Anglos*

know
Léofan menn, ʒecnáwaþ þæt sóþ is:

haste approaches
þéos weorold is on ofste and hit néalǽċþ

end therefore
þǽm ende, and þý hit is on weorolde

always the longer the worse
á swá leng swá wierse, and swá hit

by necessity Antichrist's coming
sceal níede ǽr Antecristes tócyme

become worse Understand well
yfelian swíðe. Understandaþ éac ʒeorne

devil many years led astray
þæt déofol þás þéode nú fela ʒéara dwelode

few loyalties
tó swíðe and þæt lytle ʒetríewða wǽron

among well spoke
mid mannum, þéah híe wel spǽcan; and

wrongs prevailed
unrihta tó fela ricsode on lande; and

considered about
næs á fela manna þe sméade ymbe þá

remedy
bóte swá ʒeorne swá man scolde: ac

every day (has) added
dæʒhwámlíċe man íehte yfel æfter óðrum

raised injustices
and unriht rǽrde and unlaga maniʒe

widely
ealles tó wíde ʒeond ealle þás þéode;

injuries
and wé éac for-þon habbaþ fela byrsta

insults experienced
and bismra ʒebiden.

any
And ʒief wé ǽniʒe bóte ʒebídan

must
sculan, þanne móte wé þæs tó Gode

deserve better did
earnian bet þanne wé ǽr þissum dydon;

deserts
for-þon mid miclan earnungan wé

miseries
ȝeearnodon þá iermða þe ús on sittaþ,

and mid swíðe miclan earnungan wé þá

must obtain
bóte mótan æt Gode ȝerǽċan, ȝief hit

henceforth improved
sceal heonan-forþ gódiende weorðan.

Behold!
Lá hwæt! Wé witan ful ȝeorne þæt tó

offense
miclan bryċe sceal miċel bót níede, and

burning much
tó miclum bryne wæter unlýtel, ȝief man

fire at all extinguish
þæt fýr sceal tó áhte ácwenċan. And

necessity each
miċel is níed-þearf manna ȝehwelċum

law heed
þæt hé Godes lage ȝíeme heonan-forþ

rights (i.e., tithes)
ȝeorne and Godes ȝerihta mid rihte

perform (i.e., pay)
ȝelǽste.

9.1 The comparative degree of adjectives is usually formed by adding ***-ra*** (f. and n. nom. sing. ***-re***) to the stem. It is declined as a weak adjective. The superlative (which may be declined either as weak or strong) ends in ***-ost*** (sometimes ***-est***). However, there are some adjectives which show irregularities in comparative and superlative forms: ***mára,*** for example, is actually the comparative form of ***miċel.*** Adverbs ending in ***-e*** (cf. Review Vocabulary for Chapter 6) form the comparative and superlative by adding ***-or*** and ***-ost.*** But the adverbs in the comparative degree in the passage above are all irregular: ***leng*** is the comparative of ***lange, wierse*** that of ***yfele,*** and ***bet*** that of ***wel.*** Since most such irregularities have persisted in much the same form into Mod.E., they should present little difficulty.

9.2 Of the four "anomalous" verbs (cf. section **4.5**), only forms of ***béon*** have been discussed so far, although various forms of the other three have occurred in the readings: e.g., ***dydon,*** past indicative plural of ***dón.*** Paradigms of ***dón, gán,*** and ***willan:***

Indicative

	Present			Past		
(***iċ***)	***dó***	***gá***	***wille***[1]	***dyde***	***éode***[2]	***wolde***
(***þú***)	***dést***	***gǽst***	***wilt***	***dydest***	***éodest***	***woldest***
(***hé***)	***déþ***	***gǽþ***	***wile***	***dyde***	***éode***	***wolde***
(***wé, ȝé, híe***)	***dóþ***	***gáþ***	***willaþ***	***dydon***	***éodon***	***woldon***

[1] The negative ***nyllan*** is declined like ***willan: nylle, nylt,*** etc.
[2] Note that the past forms of ***gán,*** like those of ***béon,*** come from a different root from that of the present forms.

Subjunctive

	Present			Past		
Sing., all pers.	***dó***	***gá***	***wille***	***dyde***	***éode***	***wolde***
Pl., all pers.	***dón***	***gán***	***willen***	***dyden***	***éoden***	***wolden***

9.3 A great many O.E. words are compounds formed by putting two words together—e.g., two nouns, as in ***níed-þearf*** (***níed*** 'need' + ***þearf*** 'necessity'); a preposition + a verb, as in ***néalǽċan*** (***néah*** 'near' + ***lǽċan*** 'approach') and ***understandan;*** two adverbs, as in ***heonan-forþ***—and sometimes two words of almost identical meaning are compounded, as is the case with ***níed-þearf.***

9.4 Similarly, as an adverb is often formed by adding ***-e*** or ***-líċe*** to an adjective, and an adjective by adding ***-líċ*** (among other endings) to a noun (cf. Review Vocabularies for Chapters 6 and 7), many words in O.E. are formed by adding a suffix to form a new word, as in Mod.E. Observe the relationship between the verb ***earnian*** (in the selection above) and the noun ***earnung: -ung*** is a suffix used to form a feminine abstract noun from weak II verbs. Some other common suffixes of this type are ***-dóm,*** as in ***wísdóm; -end,*** used to make a masculine noun from a participial form, as in ***Hǽlend,*** from ***hǽlan*** 'heal,' 'make whole'; ***-iʒ,*** used to form an adjective from a noun, as in ***éadiʒ,*** from ***éad*** (n.) 'wealth,' 'blessedness.'

9.5 Prefixes range from those that have relatively little effect or meaning, like ***tó-*** as in ***tócyme*** 'coming,' to those which strongly change meaning, like ***un-,*** as in ***unriht.*** Many vary considerably as to the degree of meaning; ***ʒe-,*** for example, while usually adding little if anything, sometimes has an important "perfective" significance: (***be-***)***friʒnan*** means 'ask,' but ***ʒefriʒnan*** means 'learn,' presumably by asking.

9.6 A great many O.E. nouns are derived from verbs, and vice versa: ***ricsian*** is derived from ***ríċe*** (n.) 'realm,' as is the adjective ***ríċe*** 'mighty,' 'rich'; while ***tócyme*** is derived from the verb ***(tó-)cuman.*** But note that the vowel of ***cyme*** is not the same as that of the verb from which it is derived. Similarly, ***bryne*** is derived from the verb ***beornan*** 'burn,' but there is no form of the verb that has the vowel ***y.*** Such a change in vowel is perfectly regular. It is caused by a sound change called "***i***-mutation," or "***i***-umlaut," which is the key to hundreds of such relationships: for example, the relationship of ***hǽlan*** to ***hál*** 'whole,' 'healthy.' Details of this (and other important sound changes) will be given in the next chapter.

REVIEW VOCABULARY

NOUNS

Masculine	Feminine	Neuter
bryne burning	***bót*** remedy	***éad*** wealth, blessedness
(tó-)cyme coming, arrival	***iermþu*** misery	***fýr*** fire
ende end	***þearf*** necessity	***ríċe*** realm
		riht right

PRONOUN

fela (indeclinable; also adj./adv.) much, great

ADJECTIVES

ǽniȝ any ***ȝeorn*** eager (also adv.: ***-e*** well) ***hál*** whole, healthy ***ȝehwelċ*** each, any, all ***lýtel*** small, little ***maniȝ*** many ***ríċe*** powerful ***wíde*** wide

ADVERBS

á always, ever ***forþ*** forth ***þý*** therefore ***wel*** well (comp.: ***bet***)

PREPOSITIONS

néah near ***ymb(e)*** around, about

VERBS

I: ***hǽlan*** heal, make whole
íeċan (***íehte***) increase
lǽċan approach
rǽran raise
II: ***ricsian*** rule
1: (***ʒe-)bídan*** await, experience
3: ***beornan*** (***ea, u, o***) burn
PP: ***mótan*** (***mót, móste***) may, must

EXERCISES

A. Locate in the reading selection above at least one verb (other than ***ricsian***) which is derived from a noun.

B. The genitive case is often required in O.E. in constructions where we would not use a possessive form in Mod.E. Locate as many instances of this as you can find in this selection. Can you infer any general rules (e.g., "Such-and-such a word takes the genitive")?

CHAPTER 10

The Story of Cædmon

From Bede's *Ecclesiastical History of the English People*

weak (with) age
Hé wæs ʒelýfdre ielde, and nǽfre

song learned
nǽniʒ léoþ ʒeleornode. And hé for-þon

feast
oft in ʒebéorscipe, þanne þǽr wæs

(of) merriment cause ordained
blisse intinga ʒedémed, þæt híe

in order (i.e., turn) to
ealle scolden þurh endebyrdnesse be

(the) harp
hearpan singan, þanne hé ʒeseah þá

arose
hearpan him néahlǽċan, þanne árás hé

shame banquet
for scame from þǽm symble, and hám

éode tó his húse.

Þá hé þæt þá sumre tíde dyde, þæt

hé forlét þæt hús þæs ʒebéorscipes, and

going cattle stall
út wæs gangende tó néata scipene, þára

care night
heord him wæs þǽre neahte beboden; þá

suitable limbs
hé þá þǽr in ʒelimplíċe tíde his limu on

rest slept
reste ʒesette and onslǽpte, þá stód him

by through (a) dream hailed
sum mann æt þurh swefn, and hine hálette

greeted
and grétte, and hine be his naman nemde:

something
"Cædmon, sing mé hwæt-hwugu." Þá

answered
andswarode hé and cwæþ, "Ne cann iċ

nothing
náht singan; and iċ for-þon of þissum

hither
ȝebéorscipe út éode and hider ȝewát,

for-þon iċ náht singan ne cúðe.''

Eft hé cwæþ, sé þe wiþ hine sprecende

wæs, ''Hwæðre þú mé meaht singan.''

Þá cwæþ hé, ''Hwæt sceal iċ singan?''

creation
Cwæþ hé, ''Sing mé frum-sceaft.'' Þá hé

answer began
þá þás andsware onféng, þá ongann hé

praise
sóna singan, in herenesse Godes

Creator verse
Scieppendes, þá fers and þá word þe hé

heard order
nǽfre ȝehíerde, þǽre endebyrdnesse

þis is:

(we) praise Guardian
Nú sculon herian heofon-riċes Weard,

Creator's might thought
Meotodes meahte and his mód-ʒeþanc,

Father of Glory (of) wonders each one
weorc Wuldor-Fæder, swá hé wundra ʒehwæs,

beginning established
éċe Dryhten, ór onstealde.

first (for) children
Hé ǽrest scóp eorðan bearnum

as a roof
heofon tó hrófe, háliʒ Scieppend;

earth
þá midden-ʒeard mann-cynnes Weard,

after(wards) prepared
éċe Dryhten, æfter téode

(for) men earth Lord almighty
fírum foldan, Fréa ælmihtiʒ.

sleep
þá árás hé from þǽm slǽpe, and eall

þá hé slǽpende sang fæste in ʒemynde

hæfde.

10.1 The verb (***ʒe-***)***déman*** 'judge,' 'ordain' is derived from ***dóm*** 'judgment'; the change in vowel is another example of the effects of ***i***-mutation, which means a change in vowel sound brought about by an ***i*** or ***j*** in the following syllable. Most of these ***i***'s and ***j***'s then dropped out.[1] To recognize hundreds of words derived from others, it is necessary to learn what these changes were:

Vowel mutation	Example of related words or forms
a, æ, e > e	***mann–menn***
ó > é	***dóm–déman***
á > ǽ	***hál–hǽlan***
e > i	***setl–sittan***
u > y	***burg–byriȝ***
ú > ý	***cúðe–cýðan***
ea, eo, io > ie	***eald–ieldu***
éa, éo, ío > íe	***fréond–fríend***

10.2 The effects of ***i***-mutation can be seen in the present forms of many verbs: e.g., the 3rd person singular present indicative of ***weorðan*** is often ***wierþ;*** but they do not explain why the original ***e*** of the class 3 ablaut series (cf. section **5.4**) is ***eo*** in this verb, or why the stem of the past plural and participle ends in ***-d.*** Other (mostly earlier) sound changes must also be considered. These include grammatical change by Verner's Law, change of ***a*** to ***æ,*** "breaking," and diphthongization by initial palatals.

10.3 Interchange between ***ð/d, s/r,*** and ***h/g*** in the stems of many strong verbs was caused by a change known as "Verner's Law" in words where the original stress came in a later syllable, as was the case in the past plural and past participle: e.g., ***weorðan; ċéosan, ċeas, curon, coren*** 'choose'; and ***fón*** (***féng***) (cf. section **8.4**).[2]

[1] Final ***-i*** was dropped after a long syllable, and became ***-e*** after a short syllable; medial ***i*** usually became ***e;*** and medial ***j*** was dropped after all consonants except in a short syllable ending with ***r,*** in which case it became ***i.***

[2] Verner's Law is also known as the "Second Germanic Consonant Shift." The "First Germanic Consonant Shift," known as "Grimm's Law," was that of certain Indo-European consonant sounds to those character-

10.4 ***a*** changed to ***æ*** everywhere in O.E. except before ***w, n,*** or ***m,*** or when followed by a single consonant plus ***a, o,*** or ***u.***[3] This is why ***a*** alternated with ***æ*** in the inflections of words like ***dǽʒ*** (cf. section **2.4**) and ***habban*** (cf. section **4.6**).

10.5 Some vowels became diphthongs before certain consonant groups:

> ***æ*** (< ***a***) > ***ea*** before ***h,*** or ***r*** or ***l*** + a consonant
> ***e*** and ***i*** > ***eo*** and ***io*** before ***h, lh,*** or ***r*** + a consonant

For this reason many verbs of class 3 do not show the original ***e, a*** of the ablaut series: verbs of this class always have a root syllable ending in two consonants, of which one is almost always a liquid (***l, r***) or a nasal (***m, n***). Thus we get ***weorðan, wearþ*** instead of ***werðan, warþ.***[4]

10.6 Some vowels became diphthongs when preceded by the palatal consonants ***ċ, ʒ,*** and ***sc: æ*** > ***ea, ǽ*** > ***éa, e*** > ***ie.*** Examples of this change can be seen in ***ʒiefan:*** the class 5 basic ablaut is ***e, æ, ǽ, e*** (cf. section **5.4**), but under the influence of the palatal ***ʒ*** the series becomes ***ie, ea, éa, ie.***

---

istic only of the Germanic languages; e.g., ***k*** > ***h, d*** > ***t*** (cf. Latin *cor, cordis,* O.E. ***heorte***). Among the O.E. words with apparent irregularities caused by this sound change are ***bycgan, bohte,*** and ***magan, meaht.***

[3] Single consonants, however, were often doubled later in a short syllable followed by a ***j,*** which then dropped out (cf. footnote 1, p. 66). This process is called *gemination.*

[4] A further "irregularity" in class 3 verbs, the appearance of ***i*** rather than ***e*** in the stem of many (such as ***singan***), was caused by the influence of a following nasal. Before a nasal plus a consonant, ***e*** > ***i.*** Other effects of nasals in the Primitive Germanic period were (a) to prevent the change of ***u*** > ***o***—cf. past participle ***sungen,*** but in class 3 verbs without a nasal in the stem, e.g., ***helpan,*** past participle is ***o,*** as in ***holpen;*** (b) lengthening vowels followed by ***h*** (after which the nasal dropped out)—cf. ***þynċan, þúhte.***

REVIEW VOCABULARY

NOUNS

Masculine	Feminine	Neuter
bearn[5] child, son	***bliss*** joy, bliss	***mód*** mind, spirit
dóm judgment	***folde*** earth	***wuldor*** glory
fíras men, mankind	***ieldu*** age	***wundor*** wonder, marvel
fréa lord	***meaht*** might	
fruma beginning, creation, leader		
ȝeard enclosure, yard		
meotod creator, God		
midden-ȝeard earth		
ȝeþanc thought, mind		
Scieppend Creator		
weard guardian, lord		

[5] Sometimes neuter.

PRONOUNS

ȝehwá each one ***náht*** nothing

PREPOSITIONS

ǽfter after ***þurh*** through, in, throughout (also adv.)

VERBS

I: (***ȝe-***)***déman*** judge, ordain
herian praise
(***ȝe-***)***híeran*** hear, obey
1: (***á-***)***rísan*** rise, arise
2: ***ċeosan*** (cf. section **10.3**) choose
3: (***on-***)***ȝinnan*** begin
7: ***gangen*** (***ȝéong***) go, walk

EXERCISES

A. Taking the principal sound changes into account, construct the principal parts (cf. section **5.4**) of the following strong verbs: ***scieran*** 'shear' and ***brecan*** 'break' (4); ***tredan*** 'tread' and ***ʒietan*** 'get' (5).

B. Identify the words (all to be found in the Review Vocabularies) to which the following words are related by ***i***-mutation or other sound changes: ***bearn; ǽniʒ; rǽran; wyrd*** (f.) 'fate'; ***wieldan*** (I) 'control'; ***ǽht*** (f.) 'property.' (Hints: Words based on verbs are not necessarily based on the infinitive; and, of course, there is usually an evident connection in meaning between related words.)

Appendix A

On the Meter and Form of Cædmon's Hymn

A Note on Old English Versification

The Old English verse form was based on alliteration rather than rhyme as a linking device. In each line four syllables usually receive the most important stress; at least two of these (always including the third and never—except in rare cases of a secondary, supplementary pattern—the fourth) alliterate.

These stressed syllables are not always arranged in the regularly alternating pattern that a reader accustomed to later verse forms—such as iambic pentameter—may expect. Thus, to achieve a rhythmic reading, it is necessary to observe the natural grouping of the syllables, as well as the location of the alliterating syllables; and to provide for, on the one hand, cases where two stressed syllables form one rhythmic unit (a rhythmic *measure,* to use the musical term rather than the misleading prosodic term *foot*), and, on the other hand, measures where there is no important stress at all.

The Old English verse line has two parts, referred to as either "half-lines" or *verses* (italicized terms will be used hereafter), united by alliteration. Alliteration is most often consonantal, although vocalic alliteration is frequent. Any vowel alliterates with any other, e.g., ***éċe/ór.*** While consonant clusters may be repeated (as in ***cwealm/cwén***), any initial consonant alliterates with itself alone, making possible such pairs as ***heofon/hrófe.*** However, a few clusters alliterate only as clusters: ***sc, sp,*** and ***st.*** (***Scyld Scéfing*** alliterates; ***síde scyldas*** does not.) Guttural and palatal forms of ***g*** and ***c*** are not differentiated for purposes of alliteration.

Each verse has two principal stresses or *lifts,* a lift being usually defined as a long syllable—i.e., one containing a long vowel, or ending in a long consonant (doubled in spelling) or in two or more different consonants or in a single consonant at the end of a one-syllable word: ***mann, man, ór,*** or the first syllables of ***ǽrest*** and ***æfter,*** but not the first syllable of ***heofon;*** or a stressed short syllable *resolved* into a lift with a following short syllable (***heofon*** is a resolved lift).

Syllables which are not part of lifts, whether long or short, are considered part of the *drops.* Drops range from one (or no) syllable to (in certain places of certain types of verses) five. However, in some types of verses, a *half-lift* (a syllable or resolved pair which demands heavier—secondary—stress and, in other surroundings, could be used for a lift) may substitute for, or precede or follow, a drop.

The alliteration which binds two verses into a line appears only on lifts (in some circumstances, half-lifts); only the two most important syllables (either one or both) of the first (or *on-*) verse and the first of the two most important syllables of the second (or *off-*) verse may bear alliteration. There may be an exception in the case of *crossed* alliteration, following the pattern a/b/a/b, or *transverse* alliteration, following the pattern b/a/a/b; but this is not usually considered in determining the structure of a verse. The first alliterating lift of the off-verse must in any case take precedence. Occasionally a word in a drop may alliterate with the alliterating lifts: this is not significant, and is either accidental or added decoration.

The alliterating lifts (or half-lifts) are the most important words in the line and must be words that are important logically, rhetorically, and grammatically. They are usually nouns, adjectives, infinitives, participles, or certain adverbs. Stress may be borne by other adverbs or by finite verbs, but they are more frequently displaced in importance by the parts of speech listed first above. Only under rare circumstances can prepositions, pronouns, etc., bear stress.

One or two very lightly stressed syllables may sometimes precede the first stress or drop of a verse; usually such syllables can be assigned rhythmically to the preceding verse. This is called *anacrusis,* and appears only before certain types of verses. It is not to be confused with a drop.

A verse may be rhythmically analyzed as two measures. A measure usually starts with a syllable bearing primary stress (and hence, in many cases, alliteration); however, when one measure of a verse contains both the important stressed syllables of that verse, the other measure may be composed of a *rest* and a drop. The normal measure, then, contains a lift and a drop, or a lift and a half-lift; some have a lift, a half-lift, and a drop (the order may be lift, drop, half-lift), and many substitute a rest for either the lift or the drop.

Below is Cædmon's Hymn, marked to show scansion according to these principles. Alliterating stresses are underscored. Note that such syllables are always among those bearing a stress sign, here shown by / for primary stress and \ for a second important stress within a measure which already has a primary stress. Resolved lifts are indicated by ⁀, as in ***heofon.*** In measures where there is no important stress, a pause or rest, here indicated by ∧, is necessary to complete the rhythmic interval. Bars (|) indicate measure boundaries. Each measure should be read so as to occupy about the same interval of time.

Nú sculon | herian | heofon-ríċes | Weard, ∧
Meotodes | meahte | ∧ ***and his | mód-ȝeþanc,***
weorc ∧ ***| Wuldor-Fæder, |*** ∧ ***swá hé | wundra ȝehwæs,***
éċe | Dryhten, | ór on|stealde.

∧ Hé | ǽrest scóp | eorðan | bearnum
heofon tó | hrófe, | háliʒ | Scieppend;
∧ Þá | midden-ʒeard | mann-cynnes | Weard, ∧
éċe | Dryhten, | æfter téode
fírum | foldan, | Fréa ∧ | ælmihtiʒ.

Appendix B

Forms of the Verb ***béon/wesan***

A Complete Paradigm

Indicative

		Present	Past
Sing.	(***iċ***)	***béo, eom***	***wæs***
	(***þú***)	***bist, eart***	***wǽre***
	(***hé***)	***biþ, is***	***wæs***
Pl.	(***wé, ʒé, híe***)	***béoþ, sint, sindon, earon***	***wǽron***

Subjunctive

	Present	Past
Sing., all pers.	***béo, síe, wese***	***wǽre***
Pl., all pers.	***béon, síen***	***wǽren***

Imperative

2nd per. sing.	***béo, wes***
1st per. pl.	***wuton béon, wuton wesan***
2nd per. pl.	***béoþ, wesaþ***

Present participles

béonde, wesende

Past participle

ȝebéon

Infinitives

béon, wesan

Complete Review Vocabulary

This vocabulary lists only the words which are included in the Review Vocabulary sections at the end of each chapter, plus forms of words therein included which may not be immediately recognized by the reader. The following order of the alphabet has been observed: ***a*** precedes ***æ;*** ***c*** precedes ***ċ;*** ***g*** precedes ***ȝ;*** ***t*** precedes ***þ*** (***ð*** is never initial in this book—cf. p. 4, footnote 3—medially it is treated as ***þ*** would be); and when two words are identical in spelling except for vowel length, the short vowel precedes the long one. All words with the prefix ***ȝe-*** are alphabetized under the root element, not under ***ȝ;*** other optional prefixes are similarly ignored for alphabetizing purposes, although not when the prefix actually produces a radical change in meaning. The nominative plural of nouns and the principal parts of verbs are given.

á *adv.* always, ever (cf. 'aye')
ac *conj.* but
ágan (***áh, áhst, áhte***) *PP* possess, own (cf. 'own')
ágen *adj.* own (cf. ***ágan***)
án *adj./pron.* one
and *conj.* and
andwlita (***-n***) *m.* face, appearance
(***ȝe-***)***andwyrdan*** (***andwyrde***) *I* answer (cf. ***word***)
anȝinn *n.sing.* beginning (cf. ***onȝinnan***)
ǽfre *adv.* ever
æfter *prep.* after
ǽniȝ *adj./pron.* any
ǽr *adv./conj.* before (cf. 'ere')
ǽr-þon *conj.* before
æt *prep.* at, near
æðele *adj.* noble
be *prep.* by
bearn (***-***) *m., n.* child, son
beboden see (***be-***)***béodan***

behealdan (**éo, éo, ea**) *7* behold (cf. **healdan**)
béo cf. **béon,** App. B
(**be-**)**béodan** (**éa, u, o**) *2* command
béon *A* be (cf. App. B)
beorgan (**ea, u, o**) *3* conceal, protect
beornan (**ea, u, o**) *3* burn
béoþ cf. **béon,** App. B
beran (**æ, ǽ, o**) *4* bear
bet comp. of **wel** (cf. 'better')
(**ʒe-**)**bídan** (**á, i, i**) *1* await, experience (cf. 'bide')
biddan (**bæd, bǽdon, beden**) *5* ask, pray (cf. 'bid')
biþ cf. **béon,** App. B
bliss (**-a**) *f.* joy, bliss
bót (**-a**) *f.* remedy (cf. 'boot')
(**ʒe-**)**bringan** (**bróhte**) *I* bring
bryne *m.sing.* burning (cf. **beornan**)
búgan (**éa, u, o**) *2* bow
burg (**byriʒ**) *f.* city, stronghold (cf. **beorgan**)
búton *conj.* unless, but
cann see **cunnan**
cóm see **cuman**
cuman (**ó, ó, u**) *4* come
cunnan (**cann, cannst, cúðe**) *PP* know
cúðe see **cunnan**
cweðan (**cwæþ, cwǽdon, cweden**) *5* say (cf. 'quoth')
(**tó-**)**cyme** (**-as**) *m.* coming, arrival (cf. **cuman**)
cyning (**-as**) *m.* king
cynn (**-**) *n.* race, kin, kind
cýðan (**cýðde**) *I* make known, tell, show (cf. **cúðe**)
cýðde see **cýðan**
ċeosan (**ċeas, curon, coren**) *2* choose
dæʒ (**dagas**) *m.* day
dǽl (**-as**) *m.* part (cf. **ʒedǽlan**)
(**ʒe-**)**dǽlan** (**dǽlde**) *I* divide, give out (cf. 'deal')
déaþ (**-as**) *m.* death
(**ʒe-**)**déman** (**démde**) *I* judge, ordain (cf. 'deem')
dóm (**-as**) *m.* judgment (cf. 'doom')
dón (**dyde, ʒedón**) *A* do (cf. **9.2**)
dryhten (**dryhtnas**) *m.* lord
éac *adj.* also (cf. 'eke')
éad *n.sing.* wealth, blessedness
éadiʒ *adj.* wealthy, blessed (cf. **éad**)
éage (**éagan**) *n.* eye
eald *adj.* old
ealdor (**ealdras**) *m.* lord (cf. **eald**)
eall *adj./pron.* all
eart cf. **béon,** App. B
éċe *adj.* eternal
eft *adv.* again, after, back

eȝe *m.sing.* fear
eȝeslíċe *adv.* cf. ***eȝe***
ende (***-as***) *m.* end
engel (***englas***) *m.* angel
éode see ***gán***
eom cf. ***béon,*** App. B
eorl (***-as***) *m.* noble warrior, earl
eorðe (***eorðan***) *f.* earth
éow *pron., dat. and acc.* you (cf. **2.1**)
éower *pron., gen.* your (cf. **2.1**)
faran (***ó, ó, a***) *6* go (cf. 'fare')
fæder (**-**) *m.* father
fæȝer *adj.* fair
fæst(***e***) *adj./adv.* firm(ly), fast
(***ȝe-***)***fæstnian*** (***fæstnode***) *II* fasten, secure (cf. ***fæst***)
feallan (***féoll, éo, ea***) *7* fall
fela *indeclinable pron./adj./adv.* much, greatly
féond (***-as,*** or ***fíend***) *m.* enemy (cf. 'fiend')
ȝeféra (***-n***) *m.* companion (cf. *faran*)
(***ȝe-***)***ferian*** (***ferede***) *I* carry, bring (cf. 'ferry')
fíras *m.pl.* men, mankind
folc (**-**) *n.* people, nation (cf. 'folk')
folde (***-an***) *f.* earth
(***on-***)***fón*** (***féng, féngon, fangen***) *7* grasp, take, receive
for *adv.* very (usually an intensive prefix)
for *prep.* for, on account of
forlǽtan (***é, é, ǽ***) *7* forsake (cf. ***lǽtan***)
forsácan (***ó, ó, a***) *6* forsake
for-þon *conj./adv.* because
forþ *adv.* forth, forward
fram *prep.* from, by
fréa (***-n***) *m.* lord
fréond (***-as***) *m.* friend
(***be-***) ***friȝnan*** (***fræȝn, frugnon, frugnen***) *3* inquire
fruma (***-n***) *m.* beginning, creator, leader
full *adj./adv.* full
fýr (**-**) *n.* fire
gán (***éode, éodon, ȝegán***) *A* go (cf. **9.2**)
gangen (***ȝéong, ȝéongon, gangen***) *7* go, walk (cf. 'gangway')
gást (***-as***) *m.* spirit, soul, ghost
God *m.sing.* God
gód *adj.* good
gold (**-**) *n.* gold
grimm *adj.* fierce, grim
ȝé *pron., nom.* you, ye (cf. **2.1**)
ȝeard (***-as***) *m.* enclosure, yard, dwelling
ȝearwian (***ȝearwode***) *II* prepare

ʒeond *prep.* throughout, around (cf. 'yond')
ʒeorn(e) *adj./adv.* eager(ly), well
ʒief *conj.* if
ʒiefan (ea, éa, ie) *5* give
ʒieldan (ʒeald, guldon, golden) *3* pay (cf. 'yield')
(***on-***)***ʒinnan (gann, gunnon, gunnen)*** *3* begin, undertake
ʒit *pron., nom.* you two (cf. **7.1**)
habban (hæfde, hæfd) *III* have
hál *adj.* whole, healthy (cf. 'hale')
(***ʒe-***)***hálgian (hálgode)*** *II* hallow, make holy
háliʒ *adj.* holy (cf. ***hál***)
hám (-as) *m.* home
hand (-a) *f.* hand
(***ʒe-***)***hátan (é, é, á)*** *7* call, name
hæfde see ***habban***
hǽlan (hǽlde) *I* heal, make whole (cf. ***hál***)
Hǽlend *m.sing.* savior (cf. ***hǽlan***)
hǽle (hæleðas), ***hæleþ (-)*** *m.* man, hero
hé *pron., nom.* he (cf. **5.1**)
(***ʒe-***)***healdan (éo, éo, ea)*** *7* hold
hell *f.sing.* hell
héo *pron., nom.* she (cf. **5.1**)
heofon (-as) *m.*, ***heofone (-an)*** *f.* heaven
(***ʒe-***)***héold*** cf. *healdan*
heorte (heortan) *f.* heart
hér *adv.* here
herian (herede) *I* praise
híe *pron., acc.* her; *nom./acc.* they, them (cf. **5.1**)
(***ʒe-***)***híeran (híerde)*** *I* hear, obey
him *pron., dat.* him, it, them (cf. **5.1**)
hine *pron., acc.* him (cf. **5.1**)
hira *pron., gen./dat.* her; *gen.* their (cf. **5.1**)
hit *pron., nom./acc.* it (cf. **5.1**)
hláford (-as) *m.* lord
hú *adv.* how
hús (-) *n.* house
hwá *pron., nom.* who (cf. **7.2**)
ʒehwá *pron.* each one (cf. ***hwá***)
hwæt *pron., nom.* what (cf. **7.2**); *as exclamation* Lo!, Well!
hwæðer(e) *conj./pron./adv.* whether, which, however
hwelċ *adj./pron.* which, what
ʒehwelċ *adj.* each, any, all (cf. ***hwelċ***)
hwíl (-a) *f.* while, time
iċ *pron. nom.* I (cf. **2.1**)
ídel *adj.* vain, worthless, empty (cf. 'idle')

íeċan (***íehte***) *I* increase (cf. ***éac***)

ielde *m.pl.* men, people

ieldu (***ielde***) *f.* age (cf. ***eald***)

iermþu (***iermþa***) *f.* misery

into *prep.* into

inweard *adj.* inner (cf. 'inward')

is cf. ***béon,*** App. B

land (**-**) *n.* land

lang *adj.* long

langsum *adj.* longlasting

lár (**-*a***) *f.* learning (cf. 'lore')

lǽċan (***lǽhte***) *I* approach

(***ʒe-***)***lǽdan*** (***lǽdde***) *I* lead

lǽran (***lǽrde***) *I* teach (cf. ***lár***)

lǽtan (***é, é, ǽ***) *7* permit (cf. 'let')

leng comp. of ***lang***

léod (**-*e***) *f.* nation, people

léof *adj.* dear

léoht *n.sing.* light

(***á-***)***libban*** (***lifde, lifd***) *III* live

(***á-***)***líesan*** (***líesde***) *I* set free, loose, deliver

lufian (***lufode***) *II* love (cf. ***lufu***)

lufu (***lufa***) *f.* love (cf. ***léof***)

lýtel *adj.* small, little

magan (***mæʒ, meaht/miht, meahte/mihte***) *PP* can, be able to (cf. 'may')

man *pron., impersonal* one, they

maniʒ *adj./pron.* many

mann (***menn***) *m.* man (cf. **4.3**)

má, mára *adj.* more (comp. of ***miċel***)

mæʒen (**-**) *n.* might, power (cf. 'main,' ***magan***)

mé *pron., dat./acc.* me (cf. **2.1**)

meaht see ***magan***

meaht (**-*a***) *f.* might, power (cf. ***magan***)

menn see ***mann***

mennisc *adj.* human (cf. ***mann***)

Meotod *m.sing.* Creator, God

miċel *adj.* large, much

mid *prep.* with

midd *adj.* middle

middan-ʒeard *m.sing.* earth

miht (**-*a***) *f.* might (cf. ***magan***)

mihtiʒ *adj.* mighty (cf. ***miht***)

mín *pron., gen.* my (cf. **2.1**)

mód (**-**) *n.* mind, spirit (cf. 'mood')

mótan (***mót, móst, móste***) *PP* may, must

(***ʒe-***)***munan*** (***man, manst, munde***) *PP* consider, remember

ʒemynd (**-**) *f.* mind (cf. ***munan***)

náht *pron.* nothing

nama (**-**) *m.* name

nán *adj./pron.* no, none (***ne*** plus ***án***)

nǽfre = ***ne*** plus ***ǽfre***

nǽniʒ = ***ne*** plus ***ǽniʒ***

nǽs = ***ne*** plus ***wæs*** (cf. App. B)

ne *negative particle* not, no

néah *prep.* near

néalǽċan see ***lǽcan***

neaht (**-**) *f.* night

(***ʒe-***) ***nemnan*** (***nemde***) *I* name (cf. ***nama***)

niht (**-**) *f.* night

(***ʒe-***)***niman*** (***a, á, u***) *4* take (cf. 'nimble')

nis = ***ne*** plus ***is***

nú *adv.* now

nyllan = ***ne*** plus ***willan***

of *prep.* from, of

ofer *prep.* over

oft *adv.* often

on *prep.* in, on, at

onféng see ***fón***

onfón see ***fón***

onʒietan (***ea, éa, ie***) *5* perceive

oðer *adj.* second, other

oþþe *conj.* or

rǽdan (***é, é, ǽ;*** and ***rǽdde***) *7* and *I* advise, read (cf. also 'rede')

rǽran (***rǽrde***) *I* raise (cf. 'rear')

ríċe (***ríċu***) *n.* realm, kingdom

ríċe *adj.* powerful, mighty, rich

ricsian (***ricsode***) *II* rule (cf. ***ríċe***)

riht (**-**) *n.* right, law, truth

riht (***e***) *adj./adv.* right(ly), correct(ly)

(***á-***)***rísan*** (***á, i, i***) *1* rise, arise

sácan (***ó, ó, a***) *6* fight

sang (***-as***) *m.* song

sáwol (***sáwla***) *f.* soul

sceal see ***sculon***

(***ʒe-***)***scieppan*** (***scóp, scópon, scapen***) *6* create, make (cf. 'shape')

Scieppend *m.sing.* Creator (cf. ***scieppan***)

scolde see ***sculan***

scóp see ***scieppan***

sculan (***sceal, scealt, scolde***) *PP* have to, shall

sé *art./dem. pron., nom.* the, that, he (cf. **3.2**)

(***ʒe-***)***seah*** see ***séon***

séċan (***sóhte***) *I* seek

self *adj.* self, same

sellan (***sealde***) *I* give, sell

séo *art./dem. pron., nom.* the, that, she (cf. **3.2**)

(***ʒe-***)***séon*** (***seah, sáwon, sewen***) *5* see (cf. **8.4**)

setl (**-**) *n*. seat, residence (cf. ***settan***)

(*ʒe-*)***settan*** (***sette***) *I* set, place

síe cf. ***béon,*** App. B

sindon cf. ***béon,*** App. B

singan (***a, u, u***) *3* sing

sint cf. ***béon,*** App. B

(*ʒe-*)***sittan*** (***sæt, sǽton, seten***) *5* sit, possess, inhabit

siþþan *conj*. after (cf. 'since')

sóna *adv*. at once (cf. 'soon')

sóþ *adj*. true (cf. 'sooth')

sóþlíċe *adv*. truly (cf. ***sóþ***)

sprecan (***æ, ǽ, e***) *5* speak, say

standan (***stód, stódon, standan***) *6* stand

stód see ***standan***

strang *adj*. strong

sum *adj./pron*. some, (a) certain

sunu (***suna***) *m*. son

swá *adv*. so, as

swelċ(***e***) *adj./adv*. such, which, likewise

swíðe *adv*. very, greatly

tíd (**-*a***) *f*. time, season (cf. 'tide')

tó *prep./adv*. to, too

twéʒen *adj*. two (cf. 'twain')

þá *art./dem. pron., f. acc. sing., nom./acc. pl*. cf. **3.2**

þá *adv*. then

þá . . . þá *conj*. then . . . when

(*ʒe-*)***þanc*** (**-*as***) *m*. thought, mind (cf. ***þenċan***)

þanne *adv*. then, when

þára *art./dem. pron., gen. pl*. cf. **3.2**

þás *pron., f. acc. sing., nom./acc. pl*. this, these (cf. **4.1**)

þǽm *art./dem. pron., dat. pl., m. & n. dat. sing*. cf. **3.2**

þænne *conj*. than

þǽr *adv*. there

þǽre *art./dem. pron., f. gen./dat. sing*. cf. **3.2**

þæs *art./dem. pron., m. & n. gen. sing*. cf. **3.2**

þæt *art./dem. pron., nom*. the, that, it (cf. **3.2**)

þæt, þætte *conj*. that, so that, in that

þe *pron*. who, which, what

þé *pron*. thee, you (cf. **2.1**)

þéah *conj*. though

þéah hwæðere *conj./adv*. nevertheless

þearf (**-*a***) *f*. necessity

þenċan (***þóhte***) *I* think

þéod (**-*a***) *f*. people, nation

þéos *pron., f. nom. sing*. this (cf. **4.1**)

þés *pron., m. nom. sing*. this (cf. **4.1**)

þín *pron*. thy, your (cf. **2.1**)

þing (**-**) *n*. business, thing

þis *pron.* this (cf. **4.1**)

þissum *pron., dat.* this (cf. **4.1**)

þon *art./dem. pron., m. & n. instr. sing.* (cf. **3.2**)

þone *art./dem. pron., m. acc. sing.* (cf. **3.2**)

þú *pron.* thou, you (cf. **2.1**)

þurh *prep./adv.* through, throughout, in, by way of

þý *adv.* therefore

þý *art./dem. pron., m. & n. instr. sing.* cf. **3.2**

þynċan (***þúhte***) *I* seem (with *dat.*) (cf. 'methinks')

under *prep.* under

underʒietan (***ea, éa, ie***) *5* perceive, understand

up *adv.* up, upwards

úre *pron.* our (cf. **2.1**)

ús *pron.* us (cf. **2.1**)

út *adv.* out

ʒewát see (***ʒe-***)***wítan***

wæl (***walu***) *n.* slaughter, corpse (cf. '*Val*halla')

wǽre cf. ***wesan,*** App. B

wǽron cf. ***wesan,*** App. B

wæs cf. ***wesan,*** App. B

wæter (**-** or **-*u***) *n.* water

wé *pron.* we (cf. **2.1**)

(***an-***)***weald*** (**-*a***) *f.* power, control (cf. ***wealdan***)

(***ʒe-***)***wealdan*** (***éo, éo, ea***) *7* wield, rule, control

weard (**-*as***) *m.* guardian, lord (cf. 'warden')

wel *adv.* well

weliʒ *adj.* prosperous

wénan (***wénde***) *I* expect, think (cf. 'ween')

wendan (***wende***) *I* turn, return, translate (cf. 'wend')

weorc (**-**) *n.* work

weorold (**-*a***) *f.* world

weorðan (***wearþ, wurdon, worden***) *3* become, happen

wesan (***wæs, wǽron***) *A* be (cf. App. B)

wíde *adj./adv.* wide(ly)

(***ʒe-***)***wieldan*** (***wielde***) *I* rule, control (cf. 'wield')

wiers(***a***) comp. of ***yfel***

wíf (**-**) *n.* woman, wife

wiht (**-*a***) *f.* creature, being (cf. 'wight' and 'whit')

willa (**-*n***) *m.* will, wish (cf. ***willan***)

willan (***wille, wilt, wolde***) *A* wish, will (cf. **9.2**)

wine (***winas***) *m.* friend, friendly lord

winnan (***a, u, u***) *3* strive, fight (cf. 'win')

winter (***wintru***) *n.* winter (pl.: years)

wís *adj.* wise

wísdóm *m.sing.* wisdom

wit *pron.* we two (cf. **7.1**)

wita (***-n***) *m.* wise man, counselor (cf. ***witan***)

witan (***wát, wást, wisse/ wiste***) *PP* know (cf. 'wit')

(***ʒe-***)***wítan*** (***á, i, i***) *1* go, depart

wiþ *prep.* against (cf. 'fight with . . .')

wiþstandan (***-stód, -stódon, -standen***) *6* withstand (cf. ***standan***)

wlitiʒ *adj.* beautiful

word (***-***) *n.* word, message

wuldor (***-***) *n.* glory

(***ʒe-***)***wuldrian*** (***wuldrode***) *II* glorify (cf. ***wuldor***)

wundor (***-***) *n.* marvel, wonder

wundrian (***wundrode***) *II* wonder (cf. ***wundor***)

wyrċan (***worhte***) *I* work, make (cf. ***weorc***)

yfel (***-***) *n.* evil (*also adj.*)

ymb(***e***) *prep.* around, about

Supplementary Vocabulary

Words listed here are common words which occur in the text of the readings and which have derivatives (or close relations) in Mod.E. which are still so close to the O.E. forms that the O.E. words should be easily recognizable. They have been omitted from the Review Vocabulary because they do not occur frequently enough in O.E. poetry to warrant inclusion there; but they are nevertheless everyday words, as the nature of their Mod.E. descendants would suggest.

andswarian (***andswarode***) *II* answer
andswaru *f.sing.* answer
arcebiscop (***-as***) *m.* archbishop
ascian (***ascode***) *II* ask
æcer (***-as***) *m.* field, acre
ǽfen (**-**) *n.* evening
ǽlċ *adj./pron.* each
ǽmtiʒ *adj.* empty
bæcere (***bæceras***) *m.* baker
betwénan *prep./adv.* between
biscop (***-as***) *m.* bishop
bisiʒian (***bisgode***) *II* to be busy, occupy oneself
blind *adj.* blind
bóc (***béċ***) *f.* book
bróðor (***bróðru***) *m.* brother
brycg (***-a***) *f.* bridge, causeway
bufan *prep.* above
bycgan (***bohte***) *I* buy
(***be-***)***clýsan*** (***-clýsde***) *I* close (up), enclose
(***ʒe-***)***cnáwan*** (***éo, éo, a***) *7* know, recognize
cniht (***-as***) *m.* boy, young man (cf. 'knight')
(***á-***)***cwenċan*** (***cwenċte***) *I* quench, extinguish
ċeap-mann (***-menn***) *m.* merchant (cf. 'chapman,' 'cheap')
ċild (***ċildru***) *n.* child

déofol (**-**) *m.* devil
dohtor (**-**) *f.* daughter
(***on-***)***drǽdan*** (***é, é, ǽ***) *7* dread
drífan (***á, i, i***) *1* drive
durran (***dearr, dearrst, dorste***) *PP* dare
earnian (***earnode***) *II* deserve, earn
feld (***-as***) *m.* field
(***ʒe-***)***feohtan*** (***ea, u, o***) *3* fight
fers (**-**) *n.* verse
fisc (***-as***) *m.* fish
fugel (***fuglas***) *m.* fowl, bird
fúl *adj.* foul
grétan (***grétte***) *I* greet
gylt (***-as***) *m.* guilt, sin
ʒéar (**-**) *n.* year
ʒéo *adv.* formerly, of yore
ʒeocian (***ʒeocode***) *II* to yoke
ʒíet *adv.* yet, still
hearpe (***hearpan***) *f.* harp
heonan-forþ *adv.* henceforth
hider *adv.* hither
hláf (***-as***) *m.* loaf, bread
hróf (***-as***) *m.* roof
hunta (***-n***) *m.* hunter
hwæl (***hwalas***) *m.* whale
hwít *adj.* white
lagu (***laga***) *f.* law
leornian (***learnode***) *II* learn
lim (***-u***) *n.* limb
mæsse (***mæssan***) *f.* mass
módor (**-**) *f.* mother
morgan (***morgnas***) *m.* morning
munuc (***-as***) *m.* monk
níed (***-a***) *f.* need, necessity
ofercuman (***ó, ó, u***) *4* overcome
oxa (***-n***) *m.* ox
pápa (***-n***) *m.* pope
reċċeléas *adj.* reckless
restan (***reste***) *I* rest
scamu (***scama***) *f.* shame
scéap-hierde (***-hierdas***) *m.* shepherd
scip (***-u***) *n.* ship
scóh (***scós***) *m.* shoe
sealt *n.sing.* salt
seofon *adj./pron.* seven
seonu (***seonwa***) *f.* sinew
siex *adj./pron.* six
slǽpan (***é, é, ǽ***) *7* sleep
specan (***æ, ǽ, e***) *5* speak
stearc *adj.* strong, stark
stelen (***æ, ǽ, o***) *4* steal
strǽt (***-e***) *f.* street
sweostor (**-**) *f.* sister
tǽċan (***tǽhte***) *I* teach
tíma (***-n***) *m.* time
(***ʒe-***)***tríewþ*** (***-a***) *f.* truth, loyalty (cf. ‘troth’)
understandan (***-stód, -stódon, -standan***) *6* understand
wá *m.sing.* woe
waru (***wara***) *f.* ware, merchandise

Index